MW01243185

The Millennial Challenge

How to Unleash Today's Young Talent

By Darren K. Ford

ProCulture Publishing

First Edition

ISBN: 9781494859800

Contact info:

Darren@procultureconsulting.com

www.procultureconsulting.com

Dedication

This book is dedicated to all of the Millennials I've had the pleasure of working with over the years. Your energy, enthusiasm, and outlook on life are motivating and inspirational, and I look forward to seeing how your generation changes our world!

Of all the Millennials I have known, I want to call out three special ones: my sons Austin, Jared, and Jason. Each of you has given me joy and blessings throughout the last two decades and I love watching you grow into amazing young men. I am so very proud of each of you.

Finally, this book is dedicated to the mother of those three amazing Millenials, my beautiful wife of 26 years, Pat. We've made it through times of plenty and when the pantry was a bit thin. I can't imagine living through those times with anyone but you and I can't wait to see what the next 26 years bring our way.

Contents

The Millennial Challenge

How To Unleash Today's Young Talent

They combine the teamwork ethic of the Boomers with the can-do attitude of the Veterans and the technological savvy of the Xers. At first glance, and even at second glance, Generation Next may be the ideal workforce—and ideal citizens.

Ron Zemke, Claire Raines and Bob Filipczak from
Generations at Work

I bet I will get a promotion every two years, but it'll be because I earn a promotion every two years—which I'll do because I know I'm talented, because I've worked hard.

Haley (a Millennial blogger)

Introduction:
Re-thinking your view of the
Millennial generation

•••

Before you begin reading this book, take a few minutes and write down all your perceptions of the Millennial generation. I'm sure you have some, otherwise you wouldn't be reading this book. It's probably those perceptions that motivated you to read up on this age group as more and more of them report for their first day of work at your place of business.

Your perceptions may be formed from the "kids" you've seen at the mall hovered over their smart phones while oblivious to their friends sitting across the table—who, incidentally, also seem more interested in their iPhone than those sitting next to them. Or maybe you've watched young people drive down the road with music blaring while somehow managing to hold a conversation on that same smart phone. If you are a Baby Boomer or older, you may even have a Millennial living in your home and your perceptions are verified, provided, of course, that your son or daughter is an accurate representative of this unique generation.

If you wrote down your perceptions and included descriptions such as, bratty, self-entitled, lazy, arrogant, etc., keep those handy. What you read in the pages to come may confirm those perceptions. On the other hand, you may be surprised by some ideas in this book. Much of this book is born out of my own experience with Millennials. I have raised three of my own Millennials and for years have worked with high school students and watched them go on to college or attempt to make the transition into a career.

This book is not THE exhaustive work on the Millennial generation. You are probably not interested in a lengthy discussion on why they act and think the way they do and the deep-seated motivations of their psyche. These are excellent topics to explore and there are some very good books available that dive this deeply into the Millennial world. Many business professionals, however, are simply looking for suggestions and practical strategies on how to work with this emerging workforce as they increasingly assume a greater and greater percentage of their staff.

That's what The Millennial Challenge: How To Unleash Today's Young Talent is all about; providing these suggestions and strategies in a short, simple, easy-to-read format. Considering today's fast-paced business environment, the book's format was intentional — no pictures, few anecdotal stories, and just a couple of graphs and diagrams.

What you will find, though, are simple lists of management ideas and strategies you can put into practice immediately. Those simple lists help achieve the two overarching goals of The Millennial Challenge:

1. Making you a more effective manger TODAY!

2. Unleashing your Millennial talent TODAY!

So why did I ask you to list your perceptions of Millennials? Throughout the book I hope to shatter some of those perceptions, confirm others and offer some suggestions and strategies for how to leverage their strengths, retain them and shape them into future leaders. Of course, many Millennials will eventually be leaders and take over top-level positions. One estimate states that by the year 2020, Millennials will comprise 40 percent of the workforce.

In the end, if your faulty perceptions aren't challenged and adjusted to align with reality, well, you are going to have one heck of a time working with this breed of employee. So prepare yourself to not necessarily think differently about the Millennial generation, but think accurately and realistically.

To young people everything looks permanent, established – and in their eyes everything should be, needs to be changed. To older people everything seems to change, and in their view almost nothing should.

Malcolm Forbes

. . . the four generations now working side-by-side bring unique viewpoints to the table and let generation specific values guide their daily actions.

Anne Houlihan

1

The changing workplace demographics

•••

Cataclysmic changes in the workplace are taking place before our very eyes. These changes will require businesses to rethink and restructure the way they recruit, train, manage and motivate employees. I don't use the term cataclysmic loosely. The evidence is all around and occurring at a rapid pace. Consider these trends:

- Over the next decade, 40 million people will enter the workforce, about 25 million will leave the workforce, and 109 million will remain.[1]

- The leading US advocacy group for retired people, the AARP, believes that 80% of Baby Boomers will keep working full- or part-time past their current retirement age.

- The Pew Research Center predicts that Generation U (unretired) workers will fuel 93% of the growth in the US labor market through 2016.

- The youth labor force (16 to 24 year olds) is expected to increase by 15 percent over the next decade.[2]

- The population and labor force will continue to diversify, as immigration continues to account for a sizable part of population growth. Projections suggest that the Hispanic and Asian shares of the population will rise from 14 percent in 1995 to 19 percent in 2020.[3]

There was a day when a company could set policy, establish procedures and communication channels and assume that everyone on the office floor worked from the same mindset, with the same level of motivation, expectations and work ethic. The statistics above reveal that such a work environment is now a relic of the past.

The above statistics are a clear indication that the workforce both now and in the foreseeable future will be a collection of generations that defines a new dimension of diversity. As more Americans work longer, carry AARP cards and re-enter the workforce, and as the Millennial generation fights to break into a scarce job market, the impact on office dynamics, productivity, and the overall shape of business culture will be huge. Needless to say, the world of work could be in for a rough ride unless wise management rules the day.

The employment challenges of the future are great for a variety of reasons but one in particular has managers scrambling for answers: how do you manage these fresh, new, seemingly entitled recruits called Millennials, or as others call them, Generation Y, the Digital Generation, New Boomers, Echo Boomers, Generation Next, or the Net Generation? Whatever you call them, and in this book I'll refer to them as Millennials, unless you are prepared to make adjustments to your management style and adopt a win-win management approach, you're in for quite a few headaches. You may also miss opportunities to leverage what this generation has to offer the future of businesses everywhere. That is no exaggeration.

The *Millennial Challenge* will take a look at the challenges ahead as the Millennial generation merges into the workforce. The goal here is to focus on the practical side of Millennial management rather than spend page after page on general theories of why they think and act the way they do. We'll start with some of the facts that define who they are and examine the core issues all managers face when Millennials fill job vacancies. We'll answer such questions as, "So how do I train these kids or how in the world can I communicate with them?"

Think of this book more as a reference or field guide. My goal is to offer practical help in the day-to-day managerial issues other companies have faced when trying to blend this generation into an existing workforce and to tap the skills Millennials bring to the table. Companies that see this generation as bratty, spoiled, self-entitled and over-indulged adolescents will struggle to hold on to this new workforce much less take advantage of their unique skills. On the other hand, those companies that embrace the opportunities and accept the fact that this is the generation who will take over in the years to come will position themselves to attract the finest, most qualified of this generation.

In the first section we'll answer the foundational questions: who are they, why do they think, dress and act the way they do and what impact will they have on the other generations they will be "forced" to work with? In the second section, we'll cover all the essential management questions to successfully integrate the Millennials into an already existing workforce that up to this point has functioned relatively well with set policies and expectations. Sure, some of those polices will be challenged and will need to be revisited. But isn't that the nature of business over the years anyway?

The entrance of Millennials into the workforce is only the newest and next wave of constant change that businesses constantly face. My goal is that this book will help you navigate through some potentially rough waters. Are you ready? Let's begin.

Each generation goes further than the generation pre-ceding it because it stands on the shoulders of that generation.

Ronald Reagan

The older generation thought nothing of getting up at five every morning - and the younger generation doesn't think much of it either.

John J. Welsh

2

Four generations in the workplace

...

There is a unique phenomenon unfolding in today's workplace. The forces converging on employment—struggling economy, delayed retirement, longer life expectancy—have translated into a varied mix of workers under the same roof. This has always been the case to a certain extent but the differences are becoming more stark and presenting new challenges to management. Never before has there been four distinct generations working side-by-side.

Although this book is about how to manage the new, emerging workforce we call Millennials, it's important that we first understand the context in which they will be working and the unique challenges you will face in trying to manage them. It's also helpful to remember that not only will you need to adjust your management techniques to work with Millennialls, but also your seasoned veterans will need help as well lest you face continual worker conflict that will occupy the bulk of your time.

Take an imaginary stroll through a typical office complex to see what this new diversity looks like. Down one row of cubes you find desks adorned with pictures of grandkids and walls covered with training certificates documenting years of dedicated service to the company. There's a wall calendar or a massive desk mat calendar used to keep track of events, meetings and appointments. The people sitting at these desks are your Traditionalists. They've been in the workforce for years and many are wondering if they will ever retire.[1]

Across the aisle you find other desks with pictures of older children engaged in high school and college sports, graduation pictures or family vacations. You might find inspirational messages tacked above their desktop computer or pictures of their dream car or retirement home that motivates them to work hard, compete and press on. Spread out on this desk is a Day Timer or Franklin Planner used to pencil in their many commitments, meeting notes and other reminders. These are the Baby Boomers who, even though they are contemplating retirement, are still actively engaged in the workplace.

Down a bit further you see desks covered with photos of past vacations. They depict fun and adventure in extreme, exotic locations. These walls also contain images that give a window into their personalities. Rock stars, actors and other celebrities who espouse a certain attitude or angst. Family pictures include their young children involved in all sorts of activities. With spouses decked out in fancy clothes around luxury cars made affordable by the dual incomes. There is a wall calendar but that's only there because it was a gift from a client. This occupant keeps track of important dates and appointments via Microsoft Outlook. This workstation belongs to your typical Generation X'er.

Finally, you come to completely customized workstations that are uniquely different than the previous ones. There are no family pictures plastered on the walls. Those are reserved for Facebook, Instagram, Twitter, Flickr, or some other mobile photo-sharing site. If you do get a glimpse of those photos taken with a smart phone, they might be family pictures but most consist of friends hanging out in various social settings. You won't find a planning calendar of any sort on the desk because those tools reside on their iPhone or Android device. Most likely no one is sitting at the desk because they have yet to show up for work since they started their morning at Starbucks. These desks belong to the Millennials and they will be occupying more and more of the office space in the days to come.

This is a microcosm of what today's workforce looks like. Get used to it, understand it, embrace it and learn how to manage it. This multi-generational workforce will not change anytime soon. Those who fail to understand the differences and successfully meld the generations into a collaborative workgroup will never reach their—or the company's—full potential.

In Appendix One I've provided a concise breakdown of each generation to help you understand their differences. That content could easily be shared in a team or department meeting to promote an interesting discussion about the differences in perspectives each generation brings to the table. Generational descriptions are always broad in nature and many individuals will object, "I'm not like that!" However, these descriptions are drawn from numerous sources and surveys to help gain a representative profile of the various generations at work today.

Understanding the four generations in the workforce has practical implications for the day-to-day operations of any business. It's not enough to simply know the history and influences of each generation. The more important question is what it all means when the groups try to work together and accomplish something.

Considering this new phenomenon of four generations in the workplace, there is good news and bad news. First, the bad news.

Generational clash points

Conflict is nothing new to the workplace. Put two people in one room and eventually there will be conflict. However, add four generations with four perspectives on just about everything imaginable and conflict is surely to abound. Let's take a look at four generational clash points that you must address as more Millennials fill the work stations in your office.

Clash point #1: The view of work

Ask representatives of each generation to write a definition of work and you will get four very different answers.

Start with the Traditionalists. Most likely they will define work as a "place you go." Ask them what they do for a living and you'll hear, "I work AT…" Part of what shapes their view of work is the time clock.[2] They were required to punch the time clock at a precise time at a designated location. There was no such thing as an electronic or virtual time card. For some, the time card still exists, but for Traditionalists it primarily pertained to a blue collar, labor-intensive type job. But even when those same workers moved into clerical work or managerial positions, the concept of punching in still framed their view of the work day.

Baby Boomers are very familiar with the time card concept but have blurred the lines with salaried positions that are not strictly defined by the punch in/punch out hours of 8 to 5. Because Boomers tend to be highly competitive and upwardly mobile, working a mere 40-hour week means you are a slacker. It's not uncommon for a successful Baby Boomer to boast of 50, 60 or 70 hour work-weeks.[3] They also tend to recommend to younger workers, "If you want to move up in this company, you've got to put in the time. That's what work is all about!"

When Generation X joined the workforce, they reacted to the consequences of long hours and two income families by seeking a greater balance between work and life. More than any other generation they felt the pain of divorce, extended hours in childcare and the do-or-die commitment to a career. For them it wasn't so much about the amount of hours put in but the efficiency in which the work was conducted. It was quality of work and life versus quantity of work in a specific location.

Millennials take a different view of work. They think of work as "something you do" as opposed to a place you go. They view work as more of a personal mission and an opportunity to make a positive change. After all, they have been told all their lives they can do anything they set their mind to. Since work is something you do, they reason, "Can't it be done anywhere, any time?" They don't look at work in terms of being paid for their time. They want to be compensated for their services and skills. For this reason, Millennials don't get the concept of work/life balance because to them, work is life and life is work.

Now put this all into perspective. Currently, Traditionalists or Baby Boomers are generally the people who hold positions of leadership and power. They have the seniority, experience and the title to dictate the policies governing the workplace. Along comes a member of Generation X or a Millennial who doesn't get the time clock concept or the endless hours expected from every worker. Older leaders tend to follow what author John Manning calls, "surveillance management"—if the CEO or manager walks around the office and doesn't see you sitting at your assigned desk, you must not be working.

Surveillance management creates all sorts of conflict for the younger generation of workers who have a hard time showing up to work at the same time every day or even conducting all their work in one location. In a conversation with John, who worked for a company characterized for their surveillance management style, he recalled hiring a young college graduate for a job in one of their satellite facilities. Well qualified and educated for the position, the new hire only lasted six months and rarely worked a full five-day week. She showed up to work at erratic times and constantly complained that she could get more work done at Starbucks than she could sitting at her desk in the stuffy environment. That was never going to happen in a surveillance management culture. She ultimately walked away from a Communications position for which she obtained a four-year degree to become a chef.

So remember, clash point number one means that when you say, "It's time to get to work," the meaning of that statement changes from one generation to another.

Clash Point #2: Communication preferences

It's no news flash that the speed and versatility of communications has dramatically changed within the span of time that our four generations have lived. Probably the most significant shifts in the world of communication would be from analog to digital or from personal to virtual. Communications has changed not only the speed of business transactions and operations, but the very structure and nature of business culture. Here's the challenge: everybody has a preference and is often resistant to change.

For the Traditionalists, they are comfortable with formal, written communications—memos, letters, and reports. Walk into the office of a senior manager from the Traditionalist generation and you'll find file cabinets full of old memos and letters documenting past communication transactions. On a shelf somewhere in their office you may also find rows of binders from previous meetings, conferences or training classes. They haven't been opened for years but "who could throw away such valuable information?" So if you want to communicate with a Traditionalist, send a memo.

Baby Boomers have copies of memos, letters and binders as well but they quickly adapted to email and most likely have seven thousand archived emails in their Outlook folders.

However, if you want to communicate with a Baby Boomer, opt for face-to-face. They love meetings and want people sitting across the table for discussions, reports, presentations and brainstorming. Email is good but face-to-face is serious communication where "things really get done." If you miss the meeting, you miss out on critical communication.

The younger generations, both Generation X and Y (Millennials), are much more comfortable with quick, immediate communication in the cyber or virtual world. Generation X can't remember not ever having email so it's second nature to them. Millennials, on the other hand, are way past email and opt for social media or text messages. A friend of mine tells the story of the frustration of trying to get responses back from the athletes on a team he coaches. "I keep sending them emails and they don't respond!" Someone finally suggested he launch a Facebook page to deliver information to his team. When he finally gave in, he enjoyed 100 percent cooperation and response.

So how does a manager communicate with his or her multi-generation workforce? Send a memo, an email, a text message, open a Facebook page or all the above? Do you demand that everybody tune into the same communication channel and live with it? There are strengths and weaknesses with each and every communication vehicle so is there a one-size-fits-all? Not really. You will most likely rely on a blended communication strategy that uses multiple communication methods.

Perhaps, though, the manager decides to work with the preferences of the younger generation and communicate via text message. Eventually he realizes that his entry-level Millennial is connected 24/7 and thinks nothing of "texting" him about ideas to improve the business AT ALL HOURS OF THE DAY! What's worse, he can't figure out the meaning of all the abbreviations in the excessive text messages. Welcome to clash point number two: the communication nightmare!

Clash Point #3: Business meetings

Here's the main point these days about meetings: physical or virtual? This of course is a relatively new question. Traditionalists, because they have been comfortable working in the same location with the entire staff and key players, think of meetings where everyone is physically present. The problem for younger workers is that for Traditionalists, meetings have to be scheduled in advance—throw out some dates, have everyone check their calendar, pick a time in the future and plan accordingly. Millennials, however, don't understand why meetings can't be spontaneous and connected via Skype if participants are in various locations. Why wait? Do it now!

When the economy ebbs and flows, meetings alternate between physical and conference calls due to travel expense. But even those meetings are planned for some date in the future. Traditionalists and Baby Boomers like physical meetings and have fond memories of additional activities included in the agenda and the hospitality hours afterwards.

Years ago when video conferencing was becoming a viable option to expensive meetings, I heard of one Traditionalist-aged manager who approved the purchase of a video conference system to the tune of $50,000. While the manager was still in charge of the branch office, for three consecutive years he opted for his leadership team to hold their annual meetings offsite in expensive locations for a price tag that far exceeded the cost of his fancy video conference equipment. The system was never used and after accumulating a deep layer of dust, was discarded seven years later, long after the manager had retired from the company.

Younger workers hold a different view. Gen Xers get annoyed with the enormous amounts of time that are wasted in meetings. They would rather opt for an email with an attachment and skip the meeting completely. They also think in terms of networking or project management software that tracks the contributions of others on team projects.

Millennials like meetings because throughout their education they worked in teams. However, to them, meetings should be spontaneous, physical or virtual. Why put it on the calendar? Why wait? Just have everyone jump on SKYPE and get the meeting started. They can even join the meeting from Starbucks and would prefer to do so.

In today's workplace, when a manager announces the need for a meeting, what images pop into the minds of your multi-generation workforce? Virtual? Physical? Planned? Spontaneous? Necessary? Good luck.

Clash Point # 4: Training

From our stroll down the office floor, you will recall seeing "certificates of completion" adorning the walls of the Traditionalists and some Baby Boomers. You probably won't find a single one on the wall of Gen Xers or Gen Ys, unless it's a B.A., B.S. or MBA. When Traditionalists or Baby Boomers seek training, they look for a class. They are comfortable sitting in a classroom situation taking notes from an instructor who covers important material included in their thick student workbook.

Ask a Gen Xer to attend a training class and watch the pained look on his or her face. "Just give me the manual and I'll figure it out." Tell a Millennial you want to send him or her to a class to cover certain skills and they'll likely ask, "Don't bother. I Googled it, completed the material, and found some additional information you should see."

Learning occurs differently for personality styles but also is approached differently by generation. Hold a single class for all the generations and the Traditionalists will sit in front and pay careful attention. The Boomers will fight to answer all the questions to show everyone up and win all the little prizes. Gen Xers will read ahead in the student guide and be three chapters beyond everyone else and the Millennials will search for the answers on Google and correct, update or add additional information to the discussion.

Choosing the best training methods for corporate settings has always been a challenge. Throw in the learning preferences of the various generations and it's anybody's guess regarding the most effective way to structure the learning process.

And now the good news: Generational common ground

In spite of the challenges employers face in their attempts to produce a productive workforce from such diverse generations, the news is not all bad. There are some attributes that all employees want regardless of their age and these attributes offer great rallying points for management. A 2008 study conducted by Randstad, a leading employment services provider, highlighted the similarities between the generations in contrast to the differences.[4] Participants in the study, which included a balanced cross section of the different generations, indicated they were all looking for similar workplace attributes. Here is a sampling of those values:

Respect employees and recognize the value they bring to the organization

Respect is not a virtue exclusively owned by any one generation. There may be differences from one generation to the next but if management begins by demonstrating respect for each employee and affirms all for the unique contributions brought to the organization, a foundation has been laid for a highly productive and mutually satisfying work environment.

Care about employees as much as customers

All employees want to be cared for by their employer. A simple analysis of the companies listed in the "Best Places to Work" will demonstrate the importance of caring for employees. Those companies that rank highest in terms of a best place to work invariably have the lowest employee turnover. Employees of all ages are reluctant to leave a company that treats them well and cares for them on the same level as they treat their customers.

Value employees' honest input on business issues

There is a universal drive for significance. Contrary to what some rigid, authoritarian managers believe, most employees want to make valuable contributions to the success of their employer. Often the first step in that process is simply to give them the opportunity to provide input into product development, service enhancements, business strategy or problem resolution. This universal drive is ageless. If all employees across the generations are given the opportunity to provide input, ownership within the company deepens and greater results are possible.

Encourage employees to be innovative thinkers

Valuing input from employees is a start. Encouraging innovative thinking takes employee participation to a whole new level. When employees feel their ideas are not only considered but greatly encouraged, a positive new dynamic emerges within the workforce. The beauty of extending this value across the generations is the diversity of ideas flavored by the different perspectives. The misfortune in many organizations is when ideas are suppressed due to fear of failure, rejection, punishment and ridicule. Failure to encourage innovative thinking impacts each generation differently. Traditionalists shift to maintenance mode and count their boring days down until retirement. Boomers become apathetic and collect their checks while never reaching their potential. Generation Xers' become more cynical and retreat to just do what's expected of them. Millennials jump ship in search of more welcoming, visionary companies.

Encourage employees to continually develop their skills

To a person, no one wants to be thought of as obsolete.

Everyone to some degree wants to be considered a valuable contributor to the ongoing success of the company. That's not possible unless there is an emphasis placed on continuous improvement and the opportunity to acquire new skills. This is especially true for Millennials who seek new challenges and quickly embrace new technologies.

Encourage a collaborative work environment

Every workplace has its hermits—those employees who are quite comfortable sitting in a back room alone at their isolated workstation. However, people are social creatures and most enjoy a collaborative work experience when the goals are clear, individual contributions are appreciated, ground rules are followed and success is recognized and appreciated. Millennials, fresh from their education environment, are used to working and learning in teams. Older generations enjoy the camaraderie of working on special projects. Providing employees with rich, collaborative work opportunities will greatly strengthen interpersonal dynamics.

Foster good relationships between supervisors and employees

It's safe to say, no one wants to work for a boss they despise. In traditional, top-down, command and control companies, there is a great chasm between management and employees. There is little freedom, input, collaboration or respect. This creates tension, anxiety, frustration, and factions which result in low productivity, poor work and high turnover.

These universal workplace values are embraced by all generations and form the foundation for a highly productive, much-desired work environment. Without these values in place, attempting to successfully meld the generations into a strong, positive workforce will be nearly impossible. Working with the differences among the generations is challenging enough, but when you add dysfunctional workplace values and archaic management styles, it's like trying to extinguish a forest fire with a flame thrower!

Twenty or thirty years from now a U.S. President will have a public record of photos and data that includes a lot of boyfriends or girlfriends and parties and so on.

Eric Schmidt,

CEO Google

A fatal flaw of business leaders today in developing strategy for the next 10, 20 and 30 years, is that they put themselves in that future with their mindset rather than the views and perspectives of the Millennials who will be in charge.

Unknown

3

The new kids on the payroll

•••

If you are reading this book, most likely you have a contingency of Millennial workers occupying space somewhere in your company. You may have seen countless articles or news reports about this young generation of workers entering the job market. You may have preconceived notions about who they are and the "trouble" that awaits you as they attempt to blend into your existing team. My goal is to help you gain an accurate understanding of this unique generation and provide you with workable strategies for tapping into the resources and strengths they have to offer.

Here's the situation as I see it: Stick to your established way of doing things, expect everyone to bend in your direction, hold firmly to what has worked for your company up to this point in terms of policies, procedures and cultural practices, and eventually you will have a shrinking pool of fresh candidates along with a growing turnover problem. On the other hand, if you realistically embrace change as an inevitable business dynamic, view these individuals as valuable additions to your company and as an opportunity to infuse fresh ideas and energy to your work environment, you will eliminate most of the friction that repels these eager young employees.

As was stated in the beginning, the Millennial generation will continue to enter the workforce in waves. They form the pool of candidates that you must draw from both now and in the future. They are NOT going away. They do in fact have much to offer and it is incumbent upon you to create a desirable workplace to attract and retain them to the benefit of your company.

Before we dive into the specific strategies for leveraging their immense skills, let's get a better understanding of who they are and what makes them unique.

Who They Are?

The Millennial generation is generally considered to be all who were born between 1984 and 2000. By most estimates, they total 76 million but that number is increasing due to immigration. According to a *Time* magazine article, approximately 10,000 Millennials turn 21 every day in America.[1] Some suspect that the Millennial generation could pass the 80-million member Baby Boom generation and will be three times the size of Generation X. In 2002-2003, the first wave of Millennials began knocking on doors looking for jobs. Every year since, one wave after another, which totaled 3.4 million Millennial graduates in 2012,[2] has been circulating resumes and checking internet-based job boards trying to get a slice of their version of the American dream in some lucrative job. PricewaterhouseCoopers, the multi-national professional services and accounting firm, estimates that by 2016, nearly 80 percent of their workforce will be comprised of Millennials.[3] They're here, more are coming and one day they will be in charge.

What shaped their thinking?

Every generation is shaped by the events occurring during their formative years. Millennials are no different. Throughout the 1990s and 2000s, the world and culture surrounding them played a key role in defining their worldview.

While Generation X is sometimes called the latch-key generation, Millennials experienced a very different family life. Millennials were raised by families in which the children took center stage. Their parents were attentive to their every move and interest. With highly structured schedules, they had little free time between lessons, sports activities, summer camps, school activities and homework. Many of them carried planning calendars to keep track of their daily schedules and now log everything on their smart phones complete with alerts to ensure they don't miss appointments.

The term "Helicopter Parents" became a mainstream term with this group. Overly involved and over-indulging parents played an active role in the schools, on the soccer fields and even on college campuses. Even into the workplace, some parents are still reluctant to cut the cord and completely release their children to make it on their own.

Considered to be the most diverse generation in history, Millennials grew up in an environment of multiculturalism. According to a study conducted by UCLA, 70 percent of college freshmen in 2001 reported that they had socialized with someone of another ethnic group in the last year compared to 67.6 percent the previous year.[4] Blending in with various ethnic groups is a normal part of life for these new workers coming to your company.

Whereas previous generations were exposed to fears of war such as World War II and Vietnam, wars fought on foreign soil, this generation grew up watching acts of terror unfold before their very eyes in their own country. The Oklahoma

City Bombing, attack on the World Trade Center and most recently the Boston Marathon bombing has brought them face to face with the threat of terror to their own lives. In addition to these atrocities, they have also witnessed numerous school shootings—Columbine High School, Virginia Tech, and Sandy Hook Elementary. They have also experienced foreign wars in Iraq and Afghanistan.

Another term for this generation is the "Net Generation." This age group cannot remember the day when the internet was non-existent. From the time they could operate a mouse, they realized their connection with the world was only a few clicks away. Globalism has never been an alien concept to the generation that grew up with MySpace, Facebook and YouTube.

The multi-careerism generation

If you attend a social gathering of Baby Boomers or Traditionalists, at some point early in the casual introductions, the question, "What do you do?" will pop up. Previous generations often identified themselves and their status with their career title or occupation. That's just not the case with Millennials. Few, if any, self-identify with only one job. These multi-taskers see themselves as multi-faceted in terms of job skills and careers and it's more about them than the company they work for.

A survey conducted by DeVry University and Harris Interactive found that 81 percent of Millennials surveyed believed they will have more jobs and careers in their lifetime than previous generations.[5] To Millennials, a successful career is defined by meaningful work, not a prestigious title. In the DeVry/Harris study, 71 percent stated that meaningful work was the most important factor to measure career success.

What is fueling this lack of commitment to a single company? According to Sandy Thompson of the Young & Rubicam

Advertising Agency, it's more about what they do than where they do it. "Life isn't all about work to them. They aren't working just to get a paycheck, but to make a difference," says Thompson. "There used to be an order in life: finish your education, go find a job, buy a house. This generation really mixes it up. They don't do things in any one order. They just do what feels right and feel [less] pressure to succeed [using the traditional career path] to get ahead."[6]

This multi-careerism also manifests itself in multiple jobs held simultaneously. Holding down a side job is not a new phenomenon but the challenge arises when the lines between the two are blurred. Some companies discourage and even forbid employees for holding second jobs citing reasons of divided loyalties, scheduling priorities and conflicts of interests. Other companies take a more relaxed approach and even recognize the benefits from the cross-pollination that occurs when Millennials, driven to make a difference wherever they are, leverage the skills and technologies they learn in other areas of employment. It's a delicate balance but with deft management, both can benefit—the company gains valuable expertise and the Millennial is much happier with his or her work life.

Their attitude toward the business world

Opinions on the meaning, value and substance of the recent Occupy Wall Street (OWS) movement vary greatly among those who weighed in on the subject. Although most of the protests, "park sitting" and bizarre behavior in some cases have passed, according to Barry Salzberg, global chief executive officer of Deloitte Touche Tohmstsu Limited, the OWS core beliefs "have stuck with tomorrow's talent." In an article for *Forbes*, Salzberg notes, "Occupy's core issue, damaged trust in business, remains strong with Millennials—strong in interviews, strong on college message boards, and strong on social networking sites. This fundamentally different recession has created a potentially fundamentally different generation."[7]

The tendency among established business leaders is to either brush off these "uninformed opinions of this self-entitled generation" or "set them straight when they come desperately looking for a job." Such a confrontational approach may work for some, but for others it's just another disheartening attack on their idealism that could be directed toward passionate, productive achievements. The good news is that when all the hype and angst are stripped away, both businesses and Millennials can discover they are actually working toward the same ends.

For all its alleged greed and profit, businesses do provide jobs, security, homes, opportunity and create breakthrough products and services that make life better for millions. Many companies have socially responsible programs in local and global communities that indeed align perfectly with the ideals of the younger generation. When Millennials are able to connect with companies on that level—how they are working to improve society—they will be more willing to join the cause and make a difference.

Salzberg also noted that in 2011 at Deloitte, 49,000 Millennials were hired on to their firm so naturally, the perspectives they brought to the company were a concern. A survey was conducted among 1,000 of these recruits to identify their opinions regarding the impact of business on society. The results may surprise you. In Salzberg's words, "We found that more than half of them believe that in the future business will have a greater impact than anyone else in solving society's biggest challenges. And 86% of them believe business will have at least as much potential as government to meet society's challenges. Clearly, taken as a whole, Millennials do not see business as a waste."[8]

Millennials believe they can change the world. They have

been told all their lives they can do anything they set their minds to. Some may laugh at the "blind optimism" for such lofty ambitions, but why would anyone want to dash those dreams and discourage them from even trying? Based on their beliefs that were seen in the survey conducted at Deloitte, they believe they can change the world fiscally and socially from within the system. Why not give them the opportunity and the tools to do so?

Remember, children are our future...and there's nothing we can do about it.

Steve Rosenfield, Comedian

There's a disconnect right now between what organizations are offering and what Millennials want.

Jamie Amaral

4

Recruiting Millennials

•••

The goal for most companies has always been to recruit talented employees, retain them and unleash them to drive business success. It's amazing what companies will do to lure the best and brightest onto their payroll. It's either that or lose some shining star to the competition where he or she will develop the next breakthrough product.

Companies are always hiring. Voluntary and involuntary turnover will always keep the Human Resources department on the hunt for new workers to fill the vacancies. According to the Office of Employment Projections, the average large U.S. company will lose 30-40 percent of its workforce due to retirement alone.[1] Add in voluntary (and involuntary) turnover and that's quite a few positions that will need to be filled.

To effectively attract Millennials during the recruiting process, companies must adopt a different mindset and revamp their marketing strategies to compete for the fresh, bright talent.

Start early

Traditionally, companies flock to universities and participate in job fairs hoping to get a shot at the top-of-the-class seniors who are about to launch their career. But why wait until their senior year? Some companies are finding success in project-based internships focused on students in their freshman and sophomore years. These internships offer many benefits. Students get a real taste of the corporate world and an assessment of their fit within the industry and your organization. If, after getting their hands dirty in the type of work aligned with their selected major, they have an epiphany and realize, "I just hate that kind of work," the experience saved many frustrations for both the company and the student.

On the other hand, when the student gets a taste of what is to come with a real-world company, it gives them a much better perspective on the relevance of their education and the company can assess the strengths of the intern for future permanent employment. Building a trusting relationship through internships can help secure a more promising future hire. Contrast this approach with the traditional interviewing process. Which approach gives you a more accurate picture of the Millennial's strengths and weaknesses? You decide.

Fish in the right pond

Job fairs have a place in the recruiting process, but unless you have established an online presence, Millennials may not even know you exist. Remember, they are also known as the Internet Generation. They will look for your blog, Twitter account, LinkedIn, and Facebook page. If they visit your blog (if you have one) and find stale content that is months or years old, they will look elsewhere. They have grown up posting comments and raising questions online. If you fail to respond to their comments in a timely manner, they'll assume you either don't care or don't monitor the channels and they will write you off as technologically archaic.

Susan Vitale, CMO of iCIMS, a talent acquisition software company, observes how Millennials collect information about a company before an interview. "When Millennial prospects want to conduct research before an interview, they might put the interviewer's name into their LinkedIn app and then browse the company's Twitter feed. They are the "Yelp Generation" that utilizes crowdsourced opinions before making decisions. Millennials desire to read unfiltered information to understand what it's really like working for a company."[2]

Just where are they going to get that unfiltered information about your company? Try this little experiment to "think like a Millennial". Log on to glassdoor.com and in the search field type in your company's name. Run the search and look at the comments posted about your company. This is exactly what Millennials are reading about your organization and it is what is shaping their opinions. You may not like what you read and consider it to be totally inaccurate. Nevertheless, perception is reality for these job-seeking Millennials and these are the tools they are using for their research.

Millennials will do their research before showing up to the interview. Whereas in the past candidates would go to the library or ask friends and neighbors about a company, now they sit at Starbucks with their smart phone and surf through all the available information that your company provides. So the question every company must answer is this: Are my social media channels telling the right story about the company that will resonate with the Internet Generation? Recruiting via social media is no longer an option—it's a necessity. And monitoring the social media channels they visit is also a necessity.

Connect through a deeper purpose

In 2011, PricewaterhouseCoopers (PwC) surveyed 4,364 university graduates about their expectations of work. The survey revealed that for U.S.-based Millennials, 70 percent would deliberately seek out employers whose corporate social responsibility values matched their own.[3] Interestingly, that number was down from 88 percent when the survey was taken in 2008. Maybe after battling five difficult years to find a job in a struggling economy they were willing to sacrifice some of their ideals. The fact remains, however, that connecting with a deeper purpose in their life's work is very important to Millennials.

It's not just about dollars to Millennials. They want to know why they should take the job you are offering. How does it fit into their overall goals? Justin Sherratt, CEO of Gawoop, Inc., notes from his own company's experience how important the sense of purpose is. "We found one of our best while he was still in university. Part of our offer to him was that we would help him network and move on if/when he outgrew us (advancement). We made it clear that our company helps people get jobs (social good). And we also made sure that we were working with cutting edge systems and software (training). These three combined far outweighed salary and perks at that time," Sherratt said. Connecting with purpose is a great way to motivate Millennials who work for you. More on this later.

Make it a "genuine" sales pitch

During difficult economic times when jobs are scarce, some companies relax on making attractive offers to potential new hires. They reason that if people are desperate for a job, they'll take whatever they can get regardless of the conditions. But what does that say about the company's view and treatment of its employees? And when economic conditions improve, what happens to those employees who were working in less than appealing environments?

In his book, *The Culturetopia Effect*, author and speaker Jason Young analyzes the aftermath of the economic recession following 9/11. At the height of the economic recovery, after years of staying put in jobs where conditions were bad and perks were removed, people left in droves to seek greener pastures.[4] At that point, those companies who looked across the office floor and saw massive vacancies had to ramp up the perks to attract new talent. The only problem was, their reputation preceded them and the Internet Generation was reading all the unflattering comments online and avoiding them like a plague.

The word genuine above is highlighted for a reason. All recruitment efforts are, in effect, sales pitches. In your attempts to attract the best and brightest talent, there are elements of sales that must take place. It's what author Daniel Pink calls "non-sales selling."[5] The genuine part of selling means that what you offer truly does exist within the walls of your company. When you outline why young recruits should join your team, describe the career progression they can expect and how they can make an impact on the company and the world as well. Make sure the perception you have created in their minds matches the reality they find when they sign on. So make your best sales pitch, just don't distort reality.

Adapt to Millennial-friendly recruiting materials

The Millennial generation is not accustomed to copy-heavy pamphlets or brochures. When they look for information about your company, they don't go to the library for stacks of printed material. They turn to Facebook, YouTube, Pintrest, Instagram, LinkedIn or other online sources. They will scour your webpage and turn first to interactive content, particularly video and other eye-catching infographics.

Take a look at your website. Does the content on your site engage a millennial viewer or do you have a talking-head video of your CEO droning on about how the company has returned value to its stock holders for several consecutive years? Fun and excitement play a significant role in Millennials' job aspirations and if your website is as boring as watching grass grow, they'll look somewhere else. Hire a web designer that understands this generation and retool your website to connect with Millennials in an engaging manner.

Your website should tell a story that is easy to follow. Give visitors a clear picture of what it is like to work for your company. Take them on a guided tour and let them meet some of the people who work there, people who actually appear to enjoy what they do for a living. If you do include your CEO, make sure he or she is coached down from a stodgy high-level corporate persona and comes across like a real living and breathing human being.

Make sure your site is optimized for smart phones and tablets. Those are the devices that many Millennials will use to connect with your company. They will also look for your Twitter account to follow the tweets sent from your firm. Millennials are very tech savvy and if your website looks like something from the dark ages of cyberspace, they will move on.

After you revamp your website, take a look at your job descriptions. Most of them are outdated, boring, vague and filled with extras such as, "and other duties as determined by department manager." Job descriptions should have high attraction value provided they are accurate expectations of the job being offered and are not a bait-and-switch type of proposition.

Formulate a recruiting message heard around the world

When you craft your recruiting message and strategy, don't just think in terms of the handful of positions you seek to fill this week or this month. Think long term. Be as concerned about the people who don't get the jobs as the ones who do, because they will talk. They won't just talk to the handful of friends in their dorm or apartment. Remember, this is the day of social media.

Suppose you hold a career day at your corporate office and invite 50 potential new hires to your daylong event. Over the course of the day, while they are in a group setting listening to various department heads talk about the joys of working for their company, hundreds of tweets are being sent from smart phones all across the auditorium. You may think you are only speaking to 50 Millennials, but your comments have been magnified to thousands who may never attend your career day but will have formulated an opinion of your company from the myriad of tweets and re-tweets.

So let's say out of the 50 invited to your career day only 10 positions are filled. What will the other 40 say about their experience? What will they say about how they were treated, what they heard and saw? They may be disappointed in not being among the few who got hired, but you certainly want them wowed by their day at the office, because they will tell their friends.

Lure them toward a rich culture

Millennials want to be a part of something big. Like most other employees of any age, they don't just want to walk in, do their job like an assembly line worker and leave. They want to feel connected to a team that is doing meaningful work. As we will see later, Millennials value a highly collaborative work environment that is defined by support, camaraderie, innovation and recognition. If that describes your company culture, emphasize that with recruits. If it doesn't, you might want to ask why and realize your culture may in fact repel Millennials once they get a taste for how things "really" are in your company.

Take them for a test drive

Effective, Millennial-friendly materials, as mentioned earlier, are one way to attract young talent, but what about inviting them in for a day or even a half day to see for themselves what life is like at your company? "But what if they don't like what they see?" Well, maybe they won't, but isn't it better to find that out up front before they start the job and quit a month later? And if they do come in for a test drive and decide "it's just not for them," learn from the experience and ask why.

The test drive can work both ways: recruits get a feel for life in your workspace and the company gets a sense of how the recruit may fit in. For example, after a couple of interviews, suppose there was a planning meeting or a brainstorming/problem solving session taking place. Invite potential candidates in to participate and observe how they relate to the rest of the group. You get a sense of what they have to offer (taking into consideration that it might be a tad bit intimidating) and they get a feel of the personalities of their possible future employer.

Promise flexibility

This will be discussed in more detail later but it bears mentioning here at this stage in the process. Consider this statement by Sara Sutton, CEO of Flexjobs: "Millennials don't want to fit their lives into an inflexible job. They'd much rather have the ability to blend their work and personal lives together in a way that makes sense for them."[6]

Flexjobs is a company that helps people find jobs suited to their work styles. On their website, their mission statement reads as follows:

To make your search for a telecommuting, part-time, freelance, or flextime job better, easier, faster, and safer.[7]

This mission statement is very consistent with the desires of Millennials entering the workforce. They are willing to do the work, just maybe not in the style it has always been done.

The work/life balance issue usually doesn't surface for a Baby Boomer or a Gen Xer until 15 or 20 years into a career. Flexibility is on the minds of Millennials from day one. A friend of mine told me about a Millennial he hired to work in a Fortune 50 company. The 100-year old company had a pretty rigid work culture that expected its employees to show up for work at the designated time, sit in their assigned seat and work alongside other employees until the end of the day. She only lasted six months and could never understand why she had to sit in her assigned seat when she could have gotten the same work done while curled up in a seat at Starbucks. She has a point.

If you allow flexible work options, let that be known up front. It makes for a very attractive selling point. Large companies such as Google, Chevron and Gap have implemented innovative ways to provide flexible work options to meet the needs and work styles of Millennials so it can be done. However, if you have strict, rigid guidelines for where, when and how work is to be conducted and just aren't willing to make any changes, prepare yourself for a lot of disgruntled Millennials and a high turnover rate. It's all about setting the right expectations!

Respond quickly

Baby Boomers can remember when you had to make a trip to the library to find the answer to a question. The only delays Millennials have ever known was the time it took their desktop computer to conduct a Google search. Now they whip out their smart phones and find answers within seconds. The point? Information has always been instantaneous for Millennials and they can't understand why it should take days or weeks to hear the decision about their employment. You can write that off as spoiled impatience, but that's the world that shaped the Millennial mind.

Delays are interpreted as indifference or simply that they are being ignored. If that is the perception they have of your company, guess what gets posted on Twitter? They also don't understand why they have to drive across town or across the country for an interview when Skype can bring them face to face (so to speak) for an interview right now. They may have a point. Don't ponder your decision too long. Just as they think something is wrong with the computer when the Google search is delayed, they think something is wrong with the company or that they blew the interview when your response is delayed.

...

In perspective...

One of the many labels assigned to the Millennial generation includes The Trophy Generation or The Self-Esteem Generation. The realization that trophies are not always distributed to everyone became a glaring reality when Millennials started their job searches in the midst of the economic crisis that began in 2008. Jobs quickly became scarce and for some Millennials, they faced rejection for the first time. Add to that the exorbitantly high student loan debt they acquired while hoping to land a lucrative job and they were positioned for massive discouragement. According to the Bureau of Labor

Statistics, the youth unemployment rate in July 2012 was 17.1 percent.[8] Those who did land jobs often found themselves stuck in positions far removed from what they hoped for with a massive amount of student loan debt weighting them down for years to come.

Some employers will jump at the chance to hire overly qualified Millennials at competitive or bargain prices because the eager young workers have no other options. But that strategy can backfire for a number of reasons. When Millennials fill roles far beneath their abilities and aspirations, they become discouraged quickly, indifferent to the task and cynical about the workplace. The downside for the company is disgruntled employees who never reach their potential and are always looking for a better opportunity. How effective will such a workgroup be in moving your company toward its goals?

Social media is another concern. As stated earlier, Millennials will talk. According to the Pew Internet Foundation's *2010 Future of the Internet* report, 75 percent of Millennials maintain an active presence on social media sites, compared to only 41% of the total online population.[9] It's part of their lives and will most likely be so for some time. They are connected to their friends and their friends' friends and so the ripple effect goes. When word spreads that working for your company is like living in employment hell, your pool of candidates for future jobs will "mysteriously" dry up.

An effective recruiting strategy to attract talented Millennials is a culture of care and accountability (which knows no generational bounds, by the way). A Millennial recruiting strategy should also be defined by clarity and authenticity—your promises MUST match what Millennials find when they join your team. You will never sustain an increasingly talented team of Millennials if your hiring process resembles a Hollywood movie back lot—authentic looking on the outside but a complete fake behind the scene.

A modern employer needs to give employees the opportunities and the tools to develop a satisfying work-life balance, and a work environment that provides personal satisfaction.

Gah Bird

We're not interested in slowly climbing the corporate ladder, and we're not interested in sacrificing our lives for a paycheck. It's all about personal growth, passion, and a fun work environment.

Ryan Healy (a Millennial)

5

Retaining Millennials

•••

If the first step is to attract talented young Millennials to your company, the second step, which is equally as important, is retaining the talent you've hired. Why is this so important? Here are the facts revealed in a *Millennial Branding* and *Beyond.com* study which included responses from hundreds of Human Resources professionals:

- More than 60 percent of Millennials leave their employer in less than three years.

- It costs between $15,000 and $25,000 to replace each Millennial lost to another company.

- The turnover rate for Millennials is 2:1 compared to older generations.

- It takes between three and seven weeks to hire a fully productive Millennial into a new role.

- 71% of companies reported that losing Millennial employees increases the workload and stress of current employees.[1]

Those statistics should sound an alarm for any company that opens the door to the waves of job-seeking Millennials. Unless decisive action is taken, the revolving door in your company could possibly fly off it's axis.

Some companies have active programs in place to combat the widespread turnover issue. These programs address relevant issues such as workplace flexibility, mentoring programs and internal hiring. All these initiatives are important and there's even more that can be done.

Provide what you promised

Company culture has already been mentioned in the previous chapter. Without a serious examination and assessment of your culture, all the flashy retention programs that you can imagine and launch may be nothing more than a coat of paint on a rusty car. If you make bold promises in the recruiting stage, your actual company culture better match those promises because it won't take long for Millennials to see the rust through the thin layer of paint. As soon as reality breaks through the façade, they quit.

A genuine assessment and adjustment of your company culture pays many dividends and should be an integral part of the ongoing dialog with all employees. If you have a culture that naturally repels Millennials due to it's highly rigid, top down, command and control leadership, that can't be fixed quickly. But unless cultural conversations take place and are translated into action strategies, your turnover problem will persist and your pool of Millennial candidates will shrink year by year.

Consider a consultant if you are too immersed in your own culture to fairly judge your environment where your internal business practices are eating away at your effectiveness and ability to retain young talent. The time and money invested will pay off in the long run, especially when you consider the high cost of turnover stated above.

Don't shoot the wounded

Young talent brings energy, enthusiasm and idealism to any organization. Bring new Millennials into your meeting, allow them to participate, and the dynamics of the old boring meetings will change before your eyes. That is until some cynical, seasoned veteran and self-appointed naysayer pulls out his fire hose and extinguishes all signs of life in the once hopeful youth.

Idealism should be unleashed, encouraged, directed and slowly matured, not squelched. Millennials are attracted to entrepreneurial environments and those environments must accept failure as a normal part of the learning and innovation process. If a culture of fear looms over employees like a thick fog, no one will be willing to attempt anything out of the norm or outside the lines. If that is the case, innovative growth will be virtually non-existent and your Millennials will be shopping around their resumes.

Failure can be expensive to a company but so can the lack of venture and experimentation. But when those failures lay the foundation for continuous learning and improvement, breakthrough ideas, products and services could emerge from the very next attempt.

Take a closer look at Google, considered to be one of the most innovative companies in the world. In an interview with Vinton Cerf, Google's Chief Internet Evangelist, at an Interop Conference, he identified two examples of how Google produces great new ideas in their culture of accepting failure.

1. Twenty percent time—Google allows their employees to spend 20 percent of their time on personal projects they feel have great potential for the company. They are allowed to just go for it and shoot higher and higher.

2. The push to analyze failure—failure is accepted but employees are encouraged to dig deeper to understand why failure occurred to position them for breakthroughs on the next attempt.[2]

If your company has a tendency to punish failure and if an atmosphere of fear permeates the floor space like a choking stench, you may not have many or any bruised Millennials cluttering the floors of your office—they've probably already left!

Be flexible

During the recruiting stage, work flexibility is one of the key selling points to attract Millennials. However, if you are going retain Millennials, you can't just be "open" to flexible work options, you have to accommodate them. Sahar Andrade, Executive Director of Sahar Consulting, provides additional insight into Millennials' desire for work flexibility. "Gen Y (Millennials) want to build parallel careers with flexibility to balance 'the other things' in their lives. In short, they want what their parents are just now achieving."[3]

Now, if you are a member of an older generation you may be thinking, "That's what we all want! Hey, pay your dues pal!" You probably spent years working in a rigid, inflexible office setting where you were considered slacking off if you weren't firmly planted in your chair where your boss could keep his or her eye on you. This old style thinking can and must be updated.

The key is to prevent your work environment from resembling a classroom situation where teachers "check for attendance." In school, daily attendance was taken to ensure students were in their proper place—sitting at their desk where learning takes place. That same model has carried over to many companies—work can only take place as long as the person is sitting in his/her workstation for 8 to 10 hours per day. Fortunately, some performance reviews now dig a little deeper than that to assess quality work. For the most part, though,many bosses still make the rounds like a teacher checking attendance, and as long as you are firmly planted at your desk, you are considered working for your pay.

Consider this: What if the person has a report, a presentation or a proposal to complete by an agreed upon deadline? Does the location really matter where the work is done as long as the deadline is met and the quality of the work meets or exceeds the expectation?

"Well, if he is sitting at Starbucks sipping a latte how do I know if the Millennial employee is really working?" you demand. You'll know as soon as the deadline expires and the finished work assignment is, or isn't, placed on your desk.

"What if they completed it in half the time and went shopping the rest of the day?" If that's the case, you might ask the employee to show others how to get their work done in less time. You may also set a shorter deadline next time. You might also ask if they found any good sales!

Offering flexible work options involves trust and a new set of performance metrics. From the example above, it's not about location. Authors Cali Ressler and Jody Thompson are founders of CultureRx and responsible for coining the term Results-Only Work Environment (ROWE). Their first book, *Why Work Sucks and How to Fix It*, was named the best book on work-life balance for 2008 by *Business Week*. On their website, www.gorowe.com, they define the meaning of

ROWE and the benefits it provides:

Results-Only Work Environment is a management strategy where employees are evaluated on performance, not presence. In a ROWE, people focus on results and only results – increasing the organization's performance while creating the right climate for people to manage all the demands in their lives . . . including work.

With ROWE:

- Teamwork, morale and engagement soar, which leads to fewer workers feeling overworked, stressed out or guilty.

- People are where they need to be, when they need to be – there is no need for schedules.

- There is no judgment on how people spend their time, so people at all levels stop wasting the company's time and money.[4]

Now the ROWE concept might sound a bit frightening and radical for your company and depending on the nature of your business, it might not work in all situations. If you are hiring retail sales clerks for a high-traffic department store, your sales people can't exactly offer assistance to browsing customers while sitting across town at the local coffee shop. It can, however, be a great fit for project or task-based work as either individual projects or team-oriented. The key is to have a manager who is goal oriented, truly understands what needs to be done, is comfortable managing people who are out-of-sight, and is able to move forward toward company objectives.

The ROWE concept can be a great means of attracting and retaining top, Millennial talent and it can also reveal who the underperformers are. Ressler and Thompson started the ROWE concept at the Best Buy corporate offices. After the approach was fully implemented, they noticed a 27 percent improvement in employee retention in their strategic sourcing and procurement team. They also discovered 10 low-performing employees who were a drain on their productivity expectations.[5]

Now before you rush out and tell your HR manager or CEO that ROWE needs to be implemented immediately if you expect to retain Millennials, there are legal considerations. Employees who are paid hourly are required by Federal law to log their time so they can be paid overtime. In some industries there may be contractual agreements with local unions that will also complicate a ROWE environment. But in situations where project-based, results-oriented work abounds, ROWE or something similar to it may be an attractive offer for Millennials seeking flexible, work-life balance options.

Encourage the entrepreneurial spirit

Here's an interesting statistic: According to a study conducted by UNC Kenan-Flagler Business School, 30 percent of Millennials started a business while in college and 35 percent have started a side business while working other jobs. A massive 92 percent of 21-24 year-olds surveyed said entrepreneurship education was vital in the new economy.[6]

That's who is knocking on your door looking for a job. They understand the value of an entrepreneur in today's economy. In his book *The Leader's Guide to Lateral Thinking Skills*, author Paul Slone stresses the need for employees to be entrepreneurs. "The goal is to turn [employees] into opportunistic entrepreneurs who are constantly looking for new ways of doing business."[7]

So if this new breed of employee known as the Millennials has strong entrepreneurial tendencies and if that is the type of employee needed in today's business climate, it seems like a perfect match.

So how do you encourage the entrepreneurial spirit in Millennials? Give them greater levels of responsibility and hold them accountable for the results. Of course, the level of responsibility grows with their ability to meet the challenges and good managers know when to nudge them along in that maturing process. If Millennials never get the opportunity to "own" a project and contribute something of their own creation, they quickly become bored and look elsewhere to satisfy their entrepreneurial urges.

As Millennials are melded into your organization, ask for their input—early and often in the process. Yes, they may be a bit green and their ideas may need to be tempered a bit with business realities, but what better way for them to grow and develop than by allowing them to test their ideas? Even if you know their suggestions are a bit idealistic, with a little guidance, let them chase them down and discover why their ideas might not yet be ready for prime time. What they learn in the process will only refine and strengthen their ideas and they will grow in the process.

Create a community

If you have a dining area or large break room in your office environment, stand at the back of the room during peak usage and take note of the demographics of the clusters of people: Are the clusters defined by age, seniority or management hierarchy, gender, race or other specific type? Do groups gather by department or is there cross-pollination taking place? Finally, are your Millennials grouped together as an age group in the last available space because all the other groups have claimed their territorial real estate? If this is what your dining area looks like, you don't have much of an integrated community.

Now granted, this is not a scientific analysis of your work group but it's a pretty good indication of a lack of communal sharing. Historically, companies talked about the dangers of silos that exist when departments within an organization keep to themselves and don't interact across the aisles. But what about interacting across the generations? This new aspect of diversity needs to be viewed as equally important as gender and race. As we will see in an upcoming chapter, Millennials have grown up collaborating in educational settings. If they are not invited into the club and respected for what they bring to the party, they feel ostracized and de-motivated to function like an entrepreneur.

For the most part, Millennials are highly social creatures as evidenced by the amount of time they spend on social media sites. When they post their comments, it is seen and read by thousands, so they are used to being heard and participating in conversations. When Millennials aren't allowed in the cliques and clubs at the office, it's as though someone "un-friended" them on Facebook—a very awkward feeling. Or to put it another way, which kids are the earliest to leave the Homecoming party—the ones who never get invited to dance. If you want to retain the Millennials you've hired, invite them to join the party.

Don't be afraid of fun

There are many companies today that are finding great value in creating an atmosphere of fun in the their workplace. At the Googleplex, employees are paid to play beach volleyball, test their skills on a rock-climbing wall or even bowl a few strikes at the bowling alley. Over at LinkedIn, foosball and ping-pong tables are available for anyone who gets tired of answering emails. Southwest Airlines, Zappos and other large companies encourage employees to have fun at work because they have discovered that happy employees are more productive and more creative.

Studies have demonstrated the positive benefits of laughter and play as a technique for reducing stress and promoting an overall sense of optimism. However, some companies still resist the playful activities that other companies have embraced. "Work is work and play should be done on your own time," they reason. So when it comes to Millennials, they will play on their own time, and they will look for a job where their co-workers don't take themselves so seriously.

Over the years companies have used many tools to gauge employee attitudes. Employee opinion surveys, pulse surveys, and job satisfaction assessments have been distributed routinely to monitor the level of employee engagement. So here's a new one. Albeit not very scientific, this "survey" could be very telling.

Stand out on the office floor periodically and listen for the frequency of laughter heard around the room. The next time you have a department meeting assign someone to keep a tally of the number of times your team laughs from the moment the meeting begins until the last agenda item has been completed. If employees aren't laughing, maybe things are too serious. Laughter is a good barometer of how relaxed and comfortable employees are in the workplace with their co-workers. If you ever have an occasion to visit a morgue, monitor the laughter heard there. Then evaluate the amount of laughter in your workplace. I'll let you make the comparison.

Create opportunities for growth and advancement

In the old school view of the corporate ladder, employees entered the workforce and anticipated years of paying their dues as they slowly ascended one rung at a time. According to a study conducted by Robert Half and Yahoo! HotJobs, half of the Millennial professionals surveyed believe they should only have to spend a couple years "paying their dues" in an entry-level position.[8]

Now those who have paid their dues may cop the "Join-the-club" attitude and tell the young workforce to learn to wait their turn. However, maybe it's time to take another look at the traditional corporate ladder and restructure a process that is more appealing to the aspirations of the new workforce. Instead of a vertical ladder, why not redesign the paradigm to look more like a zig-zag staircase or winding ramp?

Career coach Caroline Dowd-Higgins recommends this approach to retain Millennials who notoriously move from job to job. "Consider alternative titles that show incremental growth and smaller advancement opportunities until they are ready for a bigger promotion. This just might keep them in place longer and will meet their desire for career progression."[9] Part of that lateral movement can be achieved by providing additional training and development opportunities. As long as Millennials see possibilits to expand their portfolio of skills, they are more likely to stay put.

Be technologically savvy

If your company is slow to adopt new technology, you are likely to hear a lot of snide comments from the Millennials sitting in the back of the break room. There's a common joke among Baby Boomers: "I'm a little klutzy when it comes to this technology thing. I usually ask my kids to show me how to do it." And usually they do. How does that translate in the workforce? Not very well. Barkley, a marketing and communications services firm, conducted a study and found that Millennials are 2.5 times more likely to be an early adopter of technology than older generations whereas 35 percent of non-Millennials wait a year before trying a new technology.[10]

For example, traditionally older managers like to have face-to-face performance reviews with their employees. No one challenges the value of human contact in such conversations but Millennials don't understand why reviews, via Skype, can't be considered the same thing. There is face-to-face interaction, it's just made possible through a high-speed internet connection and the young worker can participate in the meeting from his apartment or the local coffee shop.

Some companies have cracked down on the use of social media in the workplace and consequently, some Millennials have left those companies in protest. Remember, this is the generation that can hardly remember when social media wasn't an integral part of their lives. Allowing time on social media sites simply isn't possible in some work environments. When possible, consider lightening up on your social media lookout.

A friend relayed a challenge a youth sports coach was having communicating with her athletes. The coach sent all communication via email and was frustrated by the lack of response and hearing her team constantly say, "I never saw your message." Less than half of the team checked their email on a regular basis. She switched over to the team's dedicated Facebook page for all updates and team communications. From that moment forward, no one ever missed an update because all were connected and checked the page regularly. Social media is a natural part of their lives.

As long as companies cling to traditional employee retention practices such as offering corner offices, fancy office furniture and impressive job titles, you will retain your older workers but the hinges on the exit door will snap from the steady stream of Millennials who seek job fulfillment elsewhere. So, revisit, rethink and restructure your view of the optimal work environment to achieve organizational goals while providing an enticing atmosphere for talented young Millennials to grow and thrive.

If you manage Millennials, your daily behavior should transmit this message: I value and trust you, am committed to helping you perform at your best, and care about the quality of your experience in this organization.

Venture Strategy blog

If you see Millennials grabbing onto an idea and doing what you like to see, blow the horn, cue the band, and shine a spotlight on it.

Jack Welch

6

Managing Millennials

•••

Ask any parent who has ever raised more than one child and they will tell you, even though they came from the same womb and grew up under the same roof, mysteriously they are all different. They might motivate one with small rewards while the other just isn't impressed with the same prize. Oh the challenges of parenting.

If you've never had the joy of raising multiple children, you'll get a hint of that experience when you attempt to manage multiple generations in the workplace. You've probably logged a few hours managing older generations and fallen into a fairly predictable pattern. As the waves of Millennials enter your workforce, your pattern is going to change. Rather, it must change.

Be a caring boss

In the survey conducted by Robert Half and Yahoo! Hot-Jobs mentioned earlier, a portrait of the Millennials "dream boss" emerged. Understanding, caring, flexible, open-minded as well as someone who is authoritative but respects, values and appreciates his or her employees.[1]

Now you might be thinking, "Doesn't everybody want a boss like that?" Well, the answer is yes. Who wants to work for a boss that is the antithesis of that description? However, Traditonalists and Baby Boomers were raised to respect the boss regardless of how overpowering his demeanor. In fact, it's quite possible that both of those generations were raised by parents who resembled an over-powering persona. So with that background and mentality, older generations stick it out with a boss who is a jerk. Not so with the younger generations and especially Millennials.

In general, Millennials were raised by parents who were more attentive, accessible and communicative. So much so, in fact, parenting experts have labeled them as "helicopter parents" due to their constant hovering over their kids from the cradle and well into young adulthood. More on this later. The point here is they are accustomed to ongoing supervision from parents, teachers and other authority figures and they expect the same type of attention from their boss. The Half/ Yahoo! HotJobs survey showed that 60 percent of Millennials want to hear from their boss once per day so you better polish your communication skills.

Millennials view a caring boss as someone who takes an interest in them and is willing to spend time with them. That's really a universal principle. The problem in the workplace, or in any arena where there are multiple generations, is people tend to gravitate to those who are most like themselves. The Traditionalists sit together and exchange pictures of their grandchildren and talk about "the good ol' days" when things were really tough. The Baby Boomers swap stories about the radical years, stock portfolio management, dream houses and retirement plans. Generation X talks about their extra-curricular activities and extreme sports. What do Millennials talk about?

As the age gap grows between older workers and young Millennials, those bosses who fail to cross generational barriers and engage in meaningful conversations with those many years their junior are perceived as distant, unapproachable and simply uncaring.

Rather than be judgmental, if older bosses would just take time to listen, pay attention and show genuine interest in the lives of Millennials, strong working relationships will develop and the young staff will be more responsive to the direction bosses provide.

Be a mentor

Offering mentoring opportunities was cited above as both a recruiting tool and a must for retaining Millennials. Now before you insist that your company create an elaborate mentoring program complete with organizational charts, curriculum, dates, goals and assessments, the important part to remember is that at its very core, mentoring is about sharing advice and information through relationships. Yes, it can happen formally through detailed programs. However, according to Jeanne C. Meister, co-author of the book, *The 2020 Workplace*, "Today's new mentorship models are more like Twitter conversations than the long-term relationships of days past. They're short-term and quite informal. And they end before it becomes a chore for either party—like moving on from a just-OK date."[2]

Some companies encourage "peer mentoring" where they gather employees in similar work situations and facilitate discussions amongst them to benefit from the variety of experiences. It actually resembles the dynamics of social media as if someone were scrolling through their Facebook account picking up nuggets of advice along the way. Then there's "speed mentoring," where mentees rapidly meet with various individuals for short, quick bursts of advice. Schools and organizations such as the University of Texas at El Paso and New York Women in Communications have used speed-mentoring events to connect experienced professionals with young, aspiring, career-oriented students seeking information that will put them on the right career trajectory. These snapshot mentoring opportunities are great because as Jeanne Meister says, "Millennials look for those critical few to help them reach their goals in as short an amount of time as possible."

So how does this translate to the workplace? The above examples are often structured and help students before they land their first job. Millennials may not be interested in a "you-n-me" buddy relationship with someone much older but they still want to glean those helpful tips and insights. If your leadership team is prepped for dispensing advice, they can look for those choice moments to offer seasoned wisdom and bits of insight that will help steer Millennials in the right direction. It really comes down to being alert to the development needs of your young employees and keeping those quick-hit mentoring opportunities front-of-mind. In this respect, mentoring becomes part of the culture and not a rigidly structured program.

One of the timeless management principles that is well suited for this style of mentoring is often referred to as "Management by walking around" (MBWA). You can use this approach in mentoring with a little preparation. In his book, *Communicate!*, author and corporate trainer John Manning emphasizes this approach as an effective communications tool. "When you practice MBWA you add more purpose to your encounters when you thoughtfully prepare key messages rather than just converse on the fly. Of course, the conversations should always be genuine and not come across as a robotic sales pitch or canned pep talk. But when you walk out of your office with a few key points you want to get across, your conversations become more strategic and productive."[3] Managers who truly care about mentoring rising young talent should always be planning for how they will nudge, coach and encourage Millennial employees to reach their full potential.

Some managers may use tracking tools to ensure they cover all the essentials with their employees. Those can be great planning and organizational tools when a manager's department has several team members. Whatever tools you use to guide you in the process, mentoring must be conducted in an organic way so that Millennials don't feel they are locked into a cookie-cutter development process that ignores their individuality.

Provide structure

No, that's not a contradiction to the discussion about mentoring as a natural outflow of the work relationships. Structure is important for Millennials but for different reasons. Millennials quite possibly may have been the busiest children in U.S. history. For years soccer moms carted them from practices to games to lessons and a whole host of activities that would fill the pages of their personal planner—the child's personal planner, not the parents. They are used to balancing all these activities while making time for their friends, posting comments on Twitter and sharing YouTube videos. They are connected 24/7 and respond to a constant stream of texts, tweets, reminders and prompts from their smart phone. They also don't equate their lives with their job. It is much bigger than that. Life hasn't slowed down since Mom shuttled them between activities. The only difference is now they are doing the driving and controlling their own schedule.

So what does this mean for the manager? Structure comes in the form of clear communication. Millennials want to know the job expectations so they can fit in all the other important activities in their lives. In providing them structure, here are the questions you must answer:

- What exactly is my job?

- When are the reports due and what information do you need from me?

- When are the meetings scheduled and what is the agenda?

- Can I attend the meeting via Skype and if not, why not?

- What are the goals you want me to reach?

- How do you determine my progress and success?

- Who are my team members and what are their cell phone numbers so I can text them with questions?

That's a good start. There may be other questions depending on the person and your work environment. There's not a lot of fluff in these questions—straight and to the point. They like the big picture so they can see how it all fits together. They want to know how their job and responsibilities impact the overall corporate operations as well as their overall life.

When you do answer these questions, be prepared to offer explanations if they don't make sense to the young woman or man. He or she may be trying to figure out when they can take off early to play in the local hockey league or a host of other life isues. They have a wide variety of interests to cram into their planner and they just want to cut to the chase.

Encourage their "conquer the world" attitude

The helicopter parents referred to earlier did indeed tell their children they could do anything they set their minds to. Now, of course, the older generation in the workplace smirks at this idealism after having been knocked down, beat up, bruised and brushed aside in the "real" world. But what attitude would you rather have permeate your company or team, the defeatist mindset that says the glass is not only half empty but is cracked and leaking, or the positive, confident mindset that is convinced can tackle any challenge? Which mindset will push the envelope and attempt breakthrough ideas, new processes and products?

There is a real emphasis on the need for innovation these days. Innovation cannot be achieved without the confidence that a solution can be and must be discovered. Innovation doesn't emerge from a broken down, tired, skeptical point of view. If you have Millennials working for you and they show up to work with that bright-eyed optimistic enthusiasm, by all means don't squash it. Channel it, but don't extinguish the flame. If they attempt something and it fails, keep them away from the naysayer who is just waiting to induct them into their cynical, bruised and battered club. Rather, encourage them. Help them learn from their failures and send them right back to keep working, exploring and believing they can and will make it work.

Millennials love challenges and grow bored quickly with routine and mundane tasks. They have the energy to explore, investigate, and innovate. They like new and different and want to know what is happening next as well as be a part of the development process. Fuel that energy and they will run through a wall for you. Especially if after running through the wall they can leave early to hang out with their friends.

Listen to their opinions

While mom was driving them to soccer practice, young Millennials engaged in adult conversation and expressed their opinions about which activities they liked or disliked, what they thought of their coach, piano teacher and former BFF (that's Best Friend Forever if you are not up on the abbreviation lingo). In school they were told their opinions mattered, were encouraged to be expressive and engage in debate.

Companies that have an unwritten policy about "paying your dues" before you are allowed to express an opinion are in for a big surprise. Companies that are mired in a command and control style of management and make a practice of putting people in their place before they've earned their stripes will not like these opinionated Millennials. They also won't retain them much past their orientation period.

Maybe their opinions need to be tempered and they need to learn the ropes before they spout off unseasoned advice and comments. On the other hand, rather than shut them up in an isolation chamber, maybe there is a better way to manage their desire to be heard. Take your typical organizational chart that places the CEO at the top with VPs, department heads, division managers, line managers and supervisors descending downward in order.

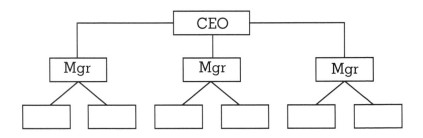

Historically, that organizational structure has a defined pecking order that all employees are expected to acknowledge, like it or not. In these companies, opinions have value relative to where they come from on the hierarchical structure. Those at the bottom don't get much of a hearing. Climb up the chart, wait your turn and then they will listen.

If your company has a top-down style organizational chart, try inverting it so the CEO is at the bottom as if he or she were holding up the entire structure.

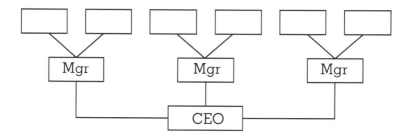

Companies that have inverted the chart figuratively and culturally are experiencing significant changes in employee morale and productivity.[4] The inverted organizational chart signifies that management's first order of business is to create a supportive environment for employees to do their best work. Companies that have adopted this approach hold the view that all employees are leaders and thus have something to contribute—even those Millennials you may think have not paid their dues. When a company changes the paradigm in favor of the inverted organizational chart, all opinions matter and should be heard. After all, insights, ideas and breakthroughs can come from anywhere.

The next time a young Millennial speaks up in a meeting or steps into your office to offer an opinion, don't roll your eyes, patronize or fire-hose his or her opinion. Welcome the opportunity to hear a perspective that you may not have considered.

Lead, don't manage

During the Industrial Revolution, the U.S. economy was heavily based on manufacturing products. That has since shifted to an information or knowledge economy where the focus is now on service—manufacturing often takes place somewhere else. However, one of the residual effects of the Industrial Revolution is the predominance of management versus leadership as the means to "get employees to do their jobs."

Companies in the Industrial Revoultion thrived when they implemented tight controls on tasks and minimized deviations. That worked well in manufacturing or for controlling workers' actions along the assembly line. In a knowledge-based economy, it's more about leadership than management and that is quite evident when it comes to working with Millennials. It is more art than science and requires the use of cognitive skills such as decision making, negotiating and problem solving.

This chapter is titled "Managing Millennials" but maybe should be titled, "Leading Millennials." The title Managing Millennials was kept because that is generally how companies approach all employees including Millennials. Leadership, on the other hand, is about outcome and results.

All employees bring a set of skills, gifts and passions to the work place. Millennials are no exception. The role of the leader is to leverage those capabilities and inspire employees to work toward the goals of the company. The manager says, "It has to be done this way." The leader says, "Together, let's figure out a better way."

Millennials have a desire to make a personal contribution that reflects their abilities. When they are forced to accomplish knowledge-based tasks in a routine and mechanical way, they lose interest, become bored and look for opportunities to make contributions in other places. They respond well to leaders who encourage and inspire them to become part of the team and create new and better ways for achieving company goals.

Managers may resist becoming a leader because it involves relinquishing control over people and processes. There is a certain amount of uncertainty when you set people free to solve problems in the absence of a step-by-step set of instructions. But those who learn to trust the skills and desires workers bring to the table witness a team that is far more motivated, fulfilled and productive than those who are told what to do, where to do it, and when to have it done.

A good leader possesses many of the qualities of a good coach. Coaches have their sights set on winning but they know every situation is different. The game plan has to change and adjust frequently in the heat of the game. They prepare their players well so when split-second decisions have to be made, they act on instinct rather that stop what they are doing, consult the playbook and then re-engage.

Great coaches know his or her players well and place them where they are most effective. A player may be lacking in certain skills but strong in other areas so the coach has realistic expectations for each team member. The coach doesn't frustrate players by pressuring them to be something they aren't.

Finally, coaches give players one-to-one attention before, during and after the game. The constant feedback is what helps the player improve his or her performance by learning from mistakes as well as successes.

Good coaches lead. They don't manage.

This is a situation that's odd and uncomfortable to say the least.

Jaime Fall

VP, HR Policy Association

I know I'm young, but at some point I have to make my own decisions.

Lauren Bailey

Millennial job seeker

7

Managing Millennials' parents

•••

In the long history of business books, you would be hard pressed to find a single chapter devoted to "managing the parents of your employees." However, when it comes to Millennials, it's a topic you can't avoid. Consider this actual scenario referred to by Steve Cody in an article for *Inc*. "Just a few weeks ago, while waiting for the elevator in our building lobby, I overheard a mother at the security desk, telling her daughter, 'Be confident, polished, and poised; they need you just as much as you need them. I'll be waiting here when you come down.'"[1]

Think that's bad? How about this one? In their book, *The M-Factor: How the Millennial Generation is Rocking the Workplace*, authors Lynne C. Lancaster and David Stillman recalled an incident about a mom who called the HR department to complain about the mediocre performance review her daughter received.[2] Like it or not, you may find that some of the Millennials who join your team are still securely attached to the umbilical cord!

Megan Huffnagle, a former human resources manager at a

Denver theme park tells this story: "An employee was hired as an IT intern, and the parent called and proceeded to tell me how talented her son was, and how he deserved much more [compensation], and that he could make much more money outside of this position."[3] What kind of parents would do this? They're called helicopter parents and you should be prepared to meet them.

Helicopter parents—those who constantly hover over their kids—follow them to college, write or edit their papers for them, review and approve their course work and attend job fairs as they near graduation.

For many, the parenting phase didn't end with graduation. Oh no. Little Johnny is not about to go off to work by himself. Authors of *The M-factor* conducted a survey for the book and found "nearly 40 percent of all respondents said they have witnessed a parent getting involved in an employee's career in a way that seemed out of line."[4] Michigan State University surveyed more than 700 employers who were looking to hire newly graduated students. They discovered that nearly one third of their parents had submitted their child's resume for them and many without their child's knowledge![5] The same study also reported that one fourth of the parents called the employer and urged the company to hire their child.

Traditionalists find this parenting style shocking. They were the generation who at 18 went off to war, came home, got married and at 20-21 years of age, accepted all the responsibilities of adulthood. Their kids, the Baby Boomers, had a little different experience. They grew up in an era of abundance and often had little contact with or perhaps a strained relationship with their parents. They grew up with the means to go to college and were immersed in a culture that was more expressive and open, one that challenged traditional values. So when it came time for Boomers to have children, the parent-child relationship was far different. They had the means to lavish the spoils of wealth on their children and were much more involved in their lives. They drove them to school, shuttled them back and forth to sports practice, music lessons and other extra-curricular activities. During all the time in the car, before the Millennials' noses were pressed against the screen of their cell phones, they talked. Now that they are at work, they still talk. And one of those parents just might call you if you are their child's boss.

Take-your-parents-to-work day

No, that section title is not a misprint. On February 15, 2013, parents of the employees working at the Googleplex were invited to "see what their kids do at work." When they opened the doors, 258 parents walked in to get an inside look at what their kids did for the tech giant. Google is widely studied for having a work culture that is attractive to young Millennials seeking a fulfilling career. They are legendary for having unusual perks including multiple fitness centers, free health clinics, free cafes and laundry services—all on site. Many companies, hoping to transform their work culture to attract rising young talent, have tried to emulate some of Google's practices. So don't be surprised when your competitors begin implementing similar programs and activities.

Google isn't the first company to host parents. In October, 2007, Ogilvy Public Relations Worldwide hosted a "Bring Your Parents to Work Day" at its New York City headquarters. However, before you think this is an event you MUST put on your company calendar to keep your Millennials happy, think again. Not all Millennials are on board with the idea. In the Wall Street Journal article that reported on the Ogilvy Public Relations parents event, most of the comments from the "kids" were not too thrilled with the idea. Consider this statement: "As much as I love my parents, I can't think of anything that would undermine my credibility at work [more] than bringing in my Mommy & Daddy to show them my desk, as if it were Parent/Teacher night at school."[6]

Don't be surprised, though, if your Millennial employee

shows up to work with a completed report, strategy, presentation or other such work assignment that has been altered, edited, revised and generally marked up by dear ol' mom or dad. They did the same with their homework assignments so why stop now? One Gen Xer found this to be the case. As he was about to leave the office for the day, the newly hired Millennial grabbed him to tell him that she had feedback on the report their team was scheduled to deliver the coming week. Her "feedback" was rather shocking to the baffled Gen Xer. "My Dad is the V.P. of Marketing at a local investment firm and he gave me a ton of ideas. He also likes your writing and only had a couple of tweaks. Otherwise, great job!"[7]

Parental involvement in the lives of their children is a good thing. Although some may take it too far, many Millennials have benefited greatly by the fact that their parents were not absent from their lives and continue to help them navigate the challenges of adulthood. Some just might need to cut the cord a little sooner than they would like.

So what should a company or a manager do? When parents do attend job fairs, show up at job interviews, call managers to extol their little darlings' strengths or take a seat at a company picnic or Christmas party, how do you handle their hovering? Well, why not use it to your advantage?

You certainly don't want to create an adversarial relationship or put a wedge between the Millennial and his or her parents. Teachers went through this as little Jennifer progressed through her school years. When teachers pushed back, parents pushed harder. Finally, teachers learned that if they took a proactive approach to involving the parents in the education process, the student ultimately benefited.

In these difficult economic times, many Millennials are living with Mom and Dad longer so they go home from work and talk about "life at the office." Those parents who go beyond listening and giving advice and who choose to pick up the phone on their child's behalf could be nudged to help their child further develop their professional skills. These are the same parents who asked the coach what Chuck needed to do to make it into the starting lineup. If you can skillfully direct the conversation, you just might be able to make an ally of the parent and in the end get a more productive and efficient employee. Of course, if this is the parent who demanded that Chuck be the starting quarterback, that's a different story.

Establish clear boundaries

It is okay to draw a line that parents can't cross. For example, Enterprise, the car rental company, sends recruitment packages to parents as well as the prospective employee because they want the involved parent to encourage the child to consider a career with the company. But when it comes time for the interview, parents are not allowed in. They express their appreciation for their interest but remind them that the child will be much better off in the long run to continue the search process on their own.[8]

There are also privacy laws that companies must follow. Regardless of how forceful a parent demands to see their child's performance review, this is an issue between HR and the employee. The Human Resources department can assist with appropriate laws and company policies and intervene when a parent tries to cross the line.

It's also important to remember that this is the generation that has grown up in the "open-source" age. They are the least likely to worry about credit card and other private information. Millennials need to be instructed regarding the proprietary information that resides on their work laptops they casually take home. It may not occur to them that when they ask their parents for help with a project, they might be exposing company information to a competitor!

Invite the folks in for a visit

If you like the "bring-your-parents-to-work day," then do it, but you might want to first poll your Millennials for their thoughts. If the overwhelming majority hates the idea, you might drop it. If they are "down for it," as they say, set it up, plan it well, and use it as a means of getting the parents to be that "unpaid tutor" who can actually help your young employees successfully transition to corporate life. If they are young in their careers, they are going to need it. Most likely their parents are Boomers who worked, or still work, with a competitive, solid work ethic. If they can encourage their child to adopt similar work habits, you will benefit in the process.

If a whole day isn't feasible, consider a special event in the evening such as an orientation for newly hired employees and encourage parents to come. It's like when the child went off to school and parents came along to meet the teacher and learn about classroom expectations, supplies needed and objectives for the school year. Yes, it sounds pretty "elementary," but if it means that you get the parents working for you, who cares?

When you think about it, for most of the Millennial generation, their parents have been and continue to be the most important people in their lives. They have guided, supported, encouraged and nurtured your young worker for years.That doesn't end when they join the workforce. Learning to leverage parents' influence in employees' work lives rather than rolling your eyes and attacking those parents head on can help transform these young employees into star performers.

In order to tap into their creative energy, we need to be respectful of the things they care about.

Dan Epstein
CEO of ReSource Pro

Millennials want and expect to be constantly excited about how they are spending their time at work.

Leader to Leader Journal

8

Motivating Millennials

•••

Millennials were raised in the self-esteem movement. The prevailing value throughout their education was to ensure they felt good about themselves. And did everyone really get a trophy, win or lose? Let's ask a Millennial first hand.

Rajpreet Heir is Social Media Strategist and Community Manager at RIVS.com, a Chicago-based digital interview software company and she is a bona fide Millennial.

"So, Rajpreet, did you really receive a ribbon for coming in 22nd out of 23 runners at your sixth grade cross country meet?"

"You bet your pension check I did. A 22nd place ribbon is burnt orange in case you were curious. We were raised with the self-esteem movement...and it shows. Our parents and teachers wanted to be our friends instead of authority figures."[1]

Now before you roll your eyes again (how many times have you done that through the first seven chapters?) and show those Millennials what life is really all about, ask who is to blame for the rise in trophy manufacturing. Parents, coaches and teachers were the ones at the finish line handing out the cheap certificates or statues regardless of how well or how poorly those Millennial competitors performed. Millennials simply became accustomed to the prize at the conclusion of the event and grew to expect it—sort of a conditioned response. This doesn't mean you need to create a new budget item and stock up on burnt orange ribbons. It does mean that you should think carefully about how you encourage and motivate all employees relative to how they are wired. And as you have seen, Millennials are wired differently.

Connect the company vision with purpose

Remember, Millennials have been told all their lives they can do anything they want. Think big. Have a vision. Change the world. Those mantras have been ringing in their ears from the day they first got a certificate for showing up to kindergarten.

So go into your corporate board room and look for the company vision printed and framed in a nice wall hanging and ask yourself this question: "Can this vision statement really and truly excite anyone about aspiring to achieve great things?" Or is it so full of jargon, fuzzy corporate-speak and trendy buzz words that if fails to even excite the CEO?

Millennials have been fed a steady diet of "Save the Planet," "World Peace," "Feed the hungry," "Free the oppressed," and other such calls to action. They have watched or participated in the Occupy Wall Street protest and identified with the need to change the perceived wrongs, greed, and abuses they are told exist in the modern world. The issue here is not whether the causes or opinions they support are informed or misguided. The point is they want to connect with a bigger purpose.

In other words, they want their work to have meaning. A 2012 Net Impact Talent report indicated that 72 percent of Millennials consider having a job where they can have an impact on a great social cause is very important or essential to their happiness.[2]

Now go back and read your company's mission and vision statement again. It may require another trip to the board room because that is generally where you'll find it. As you read the statement, is there anything in it that would link to a greater purpose beyond company growth and profit? There may be a statement or two about "industry leader in..." or "support our customers by..." but is there anything in there about strengthening communities, improving people's lives, making the world a safer place, or other such positive goals? If so, you'll be in much better position to connect with the Millennials seeking a greater purpose in their careers.

Take a cue from successful companies such as 3M and Google. 3M uses the slogan "science-based innovation to solve real-world needs." Every team member working on a 3M project knows there is a deeper purpose than simply profit involved in the success of their projects. They are in fact impacting people's lives in a positive way. Tech giant Google "organizes the world's information to make it universally accessible and useful." Millennials working at the Googleplex may like all the perks from such a game-changing work environment but at the end of the day, when they power down their PC, they know they played a part in helping people find information to make their lives better and more informed. That's connecting with purpose!

When you can connect your company's vision to making a difference in the world, make sure that vision is discussed in meetings and other conversations with not just Millennials but all employees. When people sense they are working for reasons far beyond a paycheck and a nice retirement package, they tend to work harder and with more enthusiasm and passion. When Millennials connect purpose with their career, it's what they've dreamed about and it supplies a huge surge to their motivation.

In thinking about your company's purpose, it's important to look at the bigger picture behind the widgets you make or the services you offer. Does your work improve the lives of the customers who frequent your business. For example, insurance is not just a policy State Farm sells. They view themselves as a "Good neighbor who is there." Those slogans make great pitches to potential customers but they also give employees a bigger vision for why they do what they do—"We don't sell insurance, we sell peace of mind and security." For Millennials, that connection to a larger purpose makes the difference between a job they tolerate and a job they love.

Emphasize Community Service

Many companies have seen the value of community outreach programs and global initiatives. It's good corporate citizenship to participate in worthy causes that improve the lives of people struggling with hunger, illiteracy, poverty, substance abuse and other such needs. Some companies have carefully defined, strategic philanthropic goals that include health research, support for higher education through grants and scholarships, environmental and safety issues and emergency relief. If your company has any type of programs or initiatives, by all means make that known to your Millennials—they are the most civic-minded generation of the four age groups in your office.

This is the generation that remembers watching airplanes fly into the New York City Twin Towers. They glared at their widescreen TVs and saw scores of people on rooftops waving for help in the aftermath of Hurricane Katrina. They use social media tools that are second nature to them to spread the word on crises around the world. "Community service is part of their DNA. It's part of this generation to care about something larger than themselves," says Michael Brown, co-founder and CEO of City Year, which places young mentors in urban schools. "It's no longer keeping up with the Joneses. It's helping the Joneses."[3] If they want to help the Joneses, show them the programs and opportunities your company has in place and turn them loose. In addition to being your most enthusiastic participants in volunteer activities, your Millennial workers will be proud to work for a company that supports causes important to them.

If you've ever had trouble signing up volunteers for your United Way Day of Caring or other such charitable events, look to your Millennials for help. They are volunteering in record numbers because community service is critically important to them. AmeriCorps, the domestic equivalent of the Peace Corps, has seen dramatic rises in applications, jumping from 91,399 in 2008 to 258,829 in 2010.[4] Other AmeriCorps-funded organizations such as City Year, Jumpstart, and Citizen Schools have all seen double- and triple-digit increases in applications.[5] Now many will be quick to say Millennials have flooded these organizations because in this economy they can't find jobs elsewhere. However, according to a recent *Millennial Impact Report*, 63 percent of the 6,522 people polled between the ages of 20 and 35 said they donated their time in volunteer activities.[6]

Baby Boomers recall the days of protests and demonstrations but Millennials take their passions one step further by lending a helping hand. Support their desire to have a meaningful, purposeful career by incorporating volunteerism into the work environment at your company.

Build a sense of community

Okay, true confession time. Have you ever referred to your young, newly hired Millennial employees as "rookies?" I mean to their face, in meetings or with other seasoned employees. Maybe that just seems all in fun but in a not-so-subtle way it loudly communicates, "You're the new kid. You're not part of the club yet." Think twice because these workers might resent that comment. But before you say, in the words of the Eagles song, "Get over it," and write it off because everybody was a rookie at some point in their career, think about your ultimate objective. You're looking for a productive, motivated, cohesive, supportive collection of employees all working toward the same goal. You'll never create that team spirit or sense of community if you engage in actions that alienate Millennials from the rest of the group even if it is meant as a fun, light-hearted comment.

Anthony Wolch, Executive Creative Director, Entrinsic, takes a different approach. "I have found that the key to consistently unlocking the potential of Millennials is to treat them like equals from day one. Bring them into every project. Make them sit in on more meetings than they thought possible (including client briefings, presentations, meetings with directors and producers, etc). Our youngest talent is rarely invited into the room for the meetings that provide the most insight, but I've found that instead of sheltering them, it's best to rest their future on their own shoulders and expose them to as much as possible. What you're hoping to teach them is how to get to ideas faster. It can take a little longer with younger people who aren't used to the process, but if you treat them like equals, you'll find that great ideas come from every corner of the room. The best thing about Millennials is that they come into work every day thinking they can change the world, and it's your job to let them know that they can."[7]

Building that sense of community may mean nothing more than listening to their ideas and perspectives. Good ideas can come from anywhere so it's incumbent on managers and supervisors to respect the contributions of all employees. Lose that club mentality where some people have to earn their membership.

Offer encouragement and feedback often

You're probably thinking: "Okay, now it's time for the trophies. I knew we would get to this." Before you smirk and mumble under your breath, "Those sniveling little self-entitled, trophy-happy adolescents! They got trophies even if they were on the losing team. That's just not the way it works in the real world!" remember, encouragement and feedback are universal needs that know no generational bounds.

When "thank you," "great job," and frequent pats on the back abound in the workplace, people are motivated to repeat the approved actions and rise to greater levels of excellence. Millennials are no different. True, they have been the generation that was heaped with praise from parents, teachers, coaches and other key people in their lives. But that doesn't mean encouragement has to stop now that they have entered "the real world."

One shift in your approach to feedback involves performance reviews. The corporate world is well familiar with the dreaded annual review that employees spend weeks of anxiety preparing for and weeks recovering from. Millennials though, throughout their lives, have received frequent feedback and won't be content to wait for the once-per-year assessment. "How am I doing today?" "How did I do on this project?" "What did you think of my presentation?" These are all feedback questions that can't wait until your scheduled head-to-head. And what's wrong with that? Frequent mid-course feedback and corrections keep employees encouraged, motivated and in line with company objectives.

People who resist offering encouragement and praise often do so because they fear the employee will become over-confident and arrogant. But what is the flip side of that approach? In the absence of any encouragement, people develop self-doubt, fear, anxiety and resentment toward their boss who just doesn't seem to notice when they do anything right.

A manager who is selfish with praise should also turn inward and ask if there is some personal reason why no one ever gets an "at-a-boy" (or at-a-girl). Could it be there is some deeply ingrained insecurity that says, "If I praise someone in my department for doing a good job, others might get the impression that my subordinates are smarter than me!" Managers like this have an intense need to suppress everyone else to maintain their own elevated status and sense of importance in the department. Think about it and don't let this be your mindset.

Encouragement or praise can take two forms: praise for the results or praise for the effort. Both are equally important. Think about this: Employee "A" walks into an ideal situation where an eager customer anxiously and enthusiastically signs a contract with little to no work on the part of employee "A." Meanwhile, employee "B" spends hours and hours of research, phone calls, visits, presentations, does everything exactly as she was taught in the sales training but in the end, doesn't get the sale. At the upcoming department meeting, employee "A" is recognized as "Superstar of the Month" while employee "B," who clearly worked harder than employee "A", doesn't even get a mention. Is employee "B" a failure? What is employee "B" thinking now?

Praise for results is the most obvious and easiest. If someone achieves a goal, makes a big sale, develops a new breakthrough idea, signs a new client contract, by all means, dish out the praise—especially if you want more of the same. Additinally, when a person works as hard as employee "B" yet falls short of getting the signature, praise the effort, and offer some feedback to keep the employee working with the same level of intensity. That hard work will eventually pay off.

Yes, Millennials grew up hearing all kinds of praise and yes, at times it was for no other reason than for the simple fact they wore the same uniform as all their teammates. However, just as a "one-size-fits-all" approach to anything rarely works, don't assume all employees are motivated the same way. If they need frequent encouragement and praise, if that is what motivates them to work even harder and do their best, then hand out a trophy—figuratively speaking in most cases, of course. If you appreciate their input, tell them. Even if the input was not particularly helpful or insightful, they did speak up and make an attempt, which is better than those who sit in the back of the room, contributing nothing more than sarcastic barbs and negative comments with their back -of-the-room co-workers.

If you create a work environment where praise, encouragement, and feedback are the norm, not just for Millennials but for all employees, your workplace will take on a much more positive tone and employees will enjoy a highly satisfying work experience. Your alternative is a beat down, sour group that never gets recognized unless you happen to celebrate years-of-service awards that are automatic, routine and have nothing to do with quality of service. Millennials may be labeled as the "trophy generation," but who doesn't like to get a little notice when they work hard or achieve a goal?

Develop in-between steps, titles and development opportunities

In a 2012 survey conducted by staffing agency Adecco, 68% of the recent graduates surveyed identified opportunities for growth and development as one of their top professional priorities.[8] As was discussed earlier, promotion opportunities are important to Millennials and when advancement doesn't happen fast enough, they bail in search of greener pastures. Promotion and advancement opportunities not only increase employee retention, but they also provide great motivational incentives. The question is, when the economy is stagnant and there is little movement inside the walls of an organization, how do you keep people motivated when no one is moving up? Good question.

In the retention chapter, the idea of a zig-zag or staircase progression was suggested as a new format in contrast to the proverbial corporate ladder. This is not meant to be a smoke and mirror illusion of advancement but a genuine way to reward and develop employees, including Millennials, in your company. This could include new intermediate titles that are assigned as employees demonstrate the ability to take on additional levels of responsibility. The key is that the new titles do represent changes in employee status and not just fancy, meaningless titles. If the latter is the case, the scam will be quickly detected.

There's another way to create a sense of movement within your company that could be well suited for your Millennial workforce: skill development rotations. In 2008 the Society for Human Resource Management and the Wall Street Journal conducted a study regarding the critical skills and resources needed for the changing workforce. In the study, 58 percent of HR professionals reported that some workers lacked the competencies needed to perform jobs (this deficiency was up from 54 percent in the 2005 study.[9] The research also indicated that most HR professionals felt this trend would continue for the next 10 years. Apart from the fact that schools need to do a better job equipping graduates with real-world skills, one of the conclusions reached in the study is that businesses need to implement strategies to develop skills and competencies within their current workforce.

In order of importance, here are the top skills identified

in the study considered to be necessary for new entrants in today's workforce:[10]

Skill	Priority
Adaptability / Flexibility	46%
Critical Thinking / Problem Solving	35%
Professionalism / Work Ethic	31%
Information Technology Application	30%
Teamwork / Collaboration	26%
Diversity	26%
Creativity / Innovation	25%
Written Communications	24%
Leadership	20%
Ethics / Social Responsibility	20%

As you look through this list, consider another finding from the study. Fewer than one out of ten organizations provided or paid for skills training or professional development for their U.S. workforce. Small, staff-sized organizations were even less likely to do so. Some companies might step up quickly and offer two reasons for the failure to provide needed training. First, many will say there is not time nor money to either conduct the training in-house or bring in outside trainers. Maybe there is no money in the budget but keep in mind, there is a back-side cost that results from untrained employees. Lost productivity. Inefficiencies. Low-quality work. Broken processes. So choose your poison.

The other response is, "Well, if I spend all this time and money training employees, they will leave and take their new skills somewhere else." Maybe, but what if those untrained employees stay in your company, performing far below their capabilities due to that lack of training? What a dilemma.

Let's go back to the earlier suggestion that could provide an answer for the training deficits in your company and the need for providing advancement and development opportunities for Millennials. When you think about all the projects, tasks, responsibilities, departments and various roles carried out in your company, each one may call on one or more of the skills listed above. Why not establish a rotation cycle to move employees in and out of these various functions and give them the opportunity to develop skills necessary to succeed in each job function? If they need to develop creative or innovative skills, let them work on a project in the marketing department. If they need to improve their professionalism, send them out for a while with the sales staff to see what it means to demonstrate professionalism with customers. If they lack adaptability or flexibility skills, put them on a project team that is tasked with finding solutions to real problems where there is no text book pointing to right answers.

By creating a catalog of real-world skills that all employees need and structuring a rotation cycle to move your Millennials from one area to another, you not only increase the skills of your employees, but also give them a sense of movement in and through the company that you may not be able to achieve with titles and positions. Millennials like change, opportunities to learn and new challenges. Such a structured rotation plan could play a major role in keeping motivation levels high.

What about money?

Previous generations typically heard and followed the mantra: "Get a good education to get a good job." A "good job" was defined by the amount of pay potential over the course of one's working life. Money was the big motivator in the job selection process. So is that the case for Millennials? Is that the driving force in their job selection or career aspirations?

Before that question is answered, consider the context in which Millennials find themselves as they transition into the workforce. In 2012, a Pew Research Center analysis of U.S. Census Bureau data revealed that 36 percent of the nation's Millennial generation ages 18 to 31 are living in their parents' home.[11] The contributing factors to their living arrangements are declining employment, a rise in college enrollment and a decline in marriage—unmarried Millennials are more likely to remain at home with their parents.

Those who do find jobs are accepting low-paying jobs, which makes it increasingly difficult to pay off student loans. The average student loan debt for today's Millennial is $26,000.[12] The Department of Education reports that 22 percent of college graduates are in default or forbearance with their loans. That is one in five![13] So a good portion of the Millennial generation find themselves over-educated and under-employed (if employed at all), unable to pay off their student loans, even while living at home with little living expenses. So how important is money in terms of a motivating factor? Let's see.

Most of the articles you find regarding Millennials and money state that for Millennials, it's not about the money, it's about finding fulfillment, purpose, autonomy and the opportunity to use their strengths and skills. Those are still important factors and there are many examples of Millennials leaving one company to work for another for less pay because they find the work more fulfilling. The question is, with a student loan debt hanging over their heads and less than optimal living arrangements (assuming that they do want to be on their own rather than under Mom and Dad's roof), at some point they will realize that a better income can solve a number of their financial challenges.

So if you want to motivate Millennials to become star performers, you have to put the money issue in perspective. Job fulfillment and satisfaction are still driving, motivating priorities to young Millennials. You will not be able to compensate them out their misery for a job they hate. However, it's anybody's guess when a young Millennial will awaken to the realization that money is an important factor in career aspirations. During their transition from idealism to realism, companies should continue to motivate Millennials with all the factors listed above, but also educate them on the importance of personal financial management and have open, honest conversations about wages, benefit packages and their earning potential.

Successfully motivating any employee is an ongoing learning process and in many ways requires a customized approach with each person. Managers who build strong working relationships with team members will see far greater results in motivating employees than those who apply broad generic strategies. Pay attention to your Millennial workforce and learn to speak their motivational language.

A stronger, more efficient relationship with your Gen Y employees may be just a text message away. Or, at least, a faster response time to all those voice-mails you've been leaving.

The Center for Generational Kinetics

However, in the long term, the differences can be a positive asset for a company as those situations teach employees how to deal with change.

Rosemary Haefner

Vice President of Human Resources at CareerBuilder

9

Communicating with Millennials

...

Millennials are the first generation to grow up in a world that is connected 24/7. If you have spent much time with Millennials, undoubtedly you've heard them make this statement: "How did you guys survive before there were smart phones?" That is truly a thought they cannot comprehend. Older generations perceived communication in terms of location (face-to-face), time delays (writing letters and waiting for a response) or hit or miss (call someone and hope they are near their phone). In the mind of Millennials, communication is virtually instantaneous. If you don't reply to their text message immediately, they get annoyed.

Communicating with Millennials is a broad, complex process because, let's face it, they are wired differently. Yes, that is a true statement according to a study conducted by *Time Inc.* Participants in the study involved two groups: Digital Natives, those mostly under 30 who never knew a world that was not interconnected via the internet and, Digital Immigrants, those who grew up without the internet but eventually learned to use it. Titled, *A (Biometric) Day in the Life*, the study monitored 30 participants for 10 hours a day as they went through the normal routines of their lives. Additional tools in the study included point-of-view mini-cam glasses, one-to-one interviews and a follow-up survey of 2,000 consumers of media content. Here are some of the key findings from the study:

- Digital Natives switch media platforms—divert their attention from one to another—27 times per hour, vs. Digital Immigrants who switch platforms 17 times per hour.

- Natives spend more time with media—71% of the non-work day is spent using media, vs. 64% for Immigrants.

- Natives spend about half of their media time with digital and half with non-digital media, vs. Immigrants who spend 68% of their media time with non-digital media.

- 54% of Natives prefer texting people rather than talking to them, vs. 28% of Immigrants.

- About two-thirds of Natives carry their mobile phone from room to room when they're at home vs. 41% of Immigrants.

- 66% of Natives feel that they're "naturally drawn to digital devices," while only 48% of Immigrants feel that connection.[1]

One of the conclusions drawn from the study indicated that "Because Digital Natives spend more time using multiple media platforms simultaneously, their emotional engagement with content is constrained. They experience fewer highs and lows of emotional response and as a result, Digital Natives more frequently use media to regulate their mood—as soon as they grow tired or bored, they turn their attention to something new."[2]

Dr. Carl Marci, CEO and Chief Scientist at Interscope Research, the firm that conducted the study for *Time Inc.*, noted the significance of the study's findings. "This study strongly suggests a transformation in the time spent, patterns of visual attention and emotional consequences of modern media consumption that is rewiring the brains of a generation of Americans like never before. Storytellers and marketers in this digital age will continue to face an increasingly complex environment with a higher bar for engaging an audience of consumers."[3]

So what are the implications for communicating with Millennials in the workplace? They are on and off their digital devices constantly and they send and receive text messages incessantly, any where, any time. They're posting, updating, responding, tweeting or calling at all hours of the day because they are never really disconnected. What's a manager to do?

Use technology

You have no choice—you must embrace this new communication reality. Put your foot down and say all communication should be one way such as face-to-face while in the office, and you'll drive away your young recruits. Communication has nothing to do with location and they think nothing of sending a text message to a person two cubes away. If they get bored in a meeting they will put their phone on silent and text the person on the other side of the conference room table. They are not patient enough to wait until they get face time with the boss. Why go through his or her administrative assistant when "all I need to do is ask a direct question? I'll just fire off a quick text message." Remember, they are wired differently.

If you adjust to the flexible work environment and schedules discussed earlier, you will have to include digital communications in your toolkit. For example, much is said about the proverbial "water cooler" conversations that take place on the office floor. In the traditional workplace, conversations naturally occurred in common areas when employees stepped away from their workstations for a break. Although some might perceive conversations around the water cooler as non-productive, it's those conversations that often created positive working relationships and a sense of community. How do you achieve that same dynamic in a virtual work environment or when your Millennials are pounding out their report from Starbucks?

Is there a virtual water cooler? Well, yes, and it's called Facebook, Twitter, Instagram or other social media sites. You may not connect face-to-face but to Millennials, genuine connections are made on these sites, opinions are expressed, images are shared and actual workplace contributions can be made.

Think of it this way: how often do you really cross paths at the water cooler or break room with the employees in your department? It's really hit or miss. How often do Millennials switch from one digital platform to another? According to the findings in the *Time Inc.* study, 27 times per hour! So if your Millennials are working a flexible schedule or are scattered in remote locations and you need to get the collective opinions of your team about a new service, product, issue or question, post a statement on a dedicated Facebook page and their comments will pop up much faster than their need for a cup of water from the cooler. Social networking is part of their lives. It's how they interact. These digital tools are just an extension of who they are and how they connect. If you don't join the network, you will miss valuable opportunities to communicate in a way that is meaningful to them.

This is not to say that face-to-face communication is no longer important for Millennials. Studies repeatedly show that much of communication is about tone, body language, gestures and other visual signals. You certainly can't get all that from a post on Facebook, a 140 character tweet or a brief text message. Millennials do need to learn to communicate face-to-face in team meetings, with vendors, clients and customers. But when you demand that the primary mode of communication in your company be limited to face-to-face, phone or email, you handcuff your Millennial employees from their preferred method of connecting with co-workers.

Just as there are some in your department, particularly the remaining ones from the Traditionalist generation, who still are awkward with email, there just isn't one format that is going to naturally suit everybody. For boomers and Gen Xers, email is great, maybe too great when you consider the overstuffed inboxes of many people in corporate America. Email and other forms of digital communication just don't come natural for Traditionalists and they would much rather speak in person or pick up the phone.

Millennials have grown up with texting and social media networking and are just not patient with the delayed response time that sometimes comes with email. And talking on the phone seems foreign to them. Some people, when attempting to talk to a Millennial, will place a call, get no response, leave a voice message and a few minutes later receive a text message response from the very same Millennial. Think about that. They get a call, see who it's from, and choose to ignore the call and respond almost immediately with a text message. Go figure.

Choose the right communication method

Not all communication methods are equal. Many people always fall to their favorite tool and never consider if there is a more appropriate method for a particular message to a specific group. The following grid offers suggestions on which method to use when you need to communicate an important message.

Method	When to use	When NOT to use
Email	If you need to keep a record. Short questions, meetings.	If you are typing more than two paragraphs of text.
Instant Messaging	When you are looking for a "one word answer" as well as informal communication.	When formal communication is required or more detail is needed.
Video Conferencing	When you are not able to meet face to face.	When other methods are available and you are in the same general location.
Face-to-Face Meetings	Large group needs to provide input or when you need to see body language and facial expressions.	When the information needed can be obtained by another method.
Telephone Conversations	When more than two paragraphs are required.	When short, one-word answers are needed.

Explain the "why"

Ask any Baby Boomer or Traditionalist about statements most often heard from their parents and this one usually makes the list: "Because I said so, that's why!" With that authoritative, gavel-rapping statement, older generations knew to shut up and accept it as a closed case. That's just not the case with Millennials because guess who their parents are? Those same kids grown up who vowed they would be more diplomatic and explain things in a calm sort of way. And many of them do. Millennials have generally been given thorough explanations with full descriptions of the "why" behind decisions. You may not be the boss who actually says to your employees the equivalent "Because I said so," but your lack of a clear explanation for your decisions leaves Millennials questioning your wisdom or conclusions and prevents them from buying into your leadership.

That doesn't mean that all your decisions are up for negotiation. It simply means that for Millennials, the "why's" are very important. Taking the time to explain your reasoning is an education process for them and a means to help them understand the benefits of your decisions and strategies. Communicating the "why" of your decisions also helps you examine your choices to ensure your thinking is solid and thorough. Knowing you are going to be asked "why" keeps you on your toes and forces you to avoid fuzzy, weak statements when employee buy-in is so critical.

Dialog with Millennials, not monologue

This goes hand-in-hand with answering the why questions. For the most part, Millennials are not shy. Even the ones who are hesitant to speak up prefer dialog compared to sitting with no opportunity to respond. This is the generation who is the star of their own show when it comes to expressing themselves on social media sites. They have opinions and generally don't hesitate giving them.

If you ever give a presentation, by all means make sure you allow time for questions—they'll have them. Especially if it centers on a topic that is the least bit controversial. This is the generation who didn't hear "Because I said so," and they were given the floor to discuss and debate with their parents. In the classroom they were given a voice to explore and engage in discussions as part of the discovery learning process.

Because Millennials are given to dialog over monologue, they don't fare well in a command and control, authoritarian, hierarchical management structure. If the unspoken rule in your company is "never question the leaders or even hint of challenging their decisions or strategies," your Millennials won't last long. They want to be part of the discussion, which means in their minds they should get and deserve equal time.

Don't think of this as a bratty demand resembling a temper tantrum. It's just what they experienced growing up and the idea that they can't engage in a discussion with virtually anyone in the company is just wrong to them.

Communicate early and often

For Millennials, information has always been instantaneously available. Older generations grew up waiting for the morning newspapers to hear about yesterday's news. Millennials read about or watch events as they are happening via live feeds, tweets from boots-on-the-ground or webcams placed where the action is taking place.

In the last several years companies have finally begun to wake up to the fact that the old methods of keeping employees informed are slow and inconsistent with the speed at which Millennials consume information. Look at how they are attached to their smartphones. The next time you stop at a red light in traffic, look around at others stopped at the light, particularly Millennial-aged drivers, to see how many of them use those few seconds to check their phone. Those companies that are slow to catch on often find that Millennials know about company news and announcements before the official statement from the office of the CEO—they saw it on some news feed, chat room, blog or Twitter.

Rapid communication is also important in terms of feedback. They want feedback and they don't want to wait days, weeks or next year during the annual performance review. "How am I doing right now?" is what they want to hear. Are they just being impatient? No, that's simply the world in which they live. They post a comment on Facebook and within seconds several friends "like" it. That's feedback and it's instant. They write a tweet and see how many people re-tweet it and how quickly they do so. So if they turn in a report, make a proposal or give a presentation, they want to know how they did. Did you "like" it? Tell them now.

Communication tools have changed dramatically over the last several decades but the need to connect remains just as important in spite of those changes. Regardless of the methods used or the generation with whom you are communicating, time and effort must be given to ensure mutual understanding has been achieved in every communication transaction.

If you do not provide development, it's like a slap in the face.

Jeremy Kingsley, leadership expert and author

In fact, Generation Y decides how much attention we're going to give you within the first five minutes of instruction.

Preston, a Milllennial

10

Training and developing Millennials

•••

Although the Millennial generation could be the most educated young workforce to enter corporate America in decades, their education has not completely prepared them for what they are about to encounter when they set up shop in their newly assigned work stations. They are walking away from college life where, for the most part, they created their own schedule (according to when classes were available), chose their own courses, studied on their timetable in the location of their choosing, wore what they wanted, slept when they wanted and skipped class occasionally (or frequently depending on the class and the instructor). Generally, they were master of their own destiny. At least while in college.

Think of the culture shock when they leave that world behind and enter corporate America. Traditionally there is a set schedule for working—start and end times—a set location, dress code, standards for office behavior, limits on the number of days off and warnings for tardiness. And they don't get extended summer and Christmas breaks! They may have learned accounting principles or marketing strategies but chances are they are in for a big surprise when it comes to adapting to the office policies of their new environment.

The more hard-core Traditionalists, Baby Boomers and Gen Xers, might be inclined to say, "Get over it and get to work! We've all had to learn to adjust." That might work for some but for others, the "trauma" these new employees encounter might be so jarring they go through several job attempts before they acclimate to this new world. Companies can assist in this transition if they view the employee development process more broadly than just training them in specific job skills and responsibilities.

Orientation to your company's culture

Most companies have some type of new employee orientation. They want these employees to understand the history, values, goals and opportunities of working for "this great company you've joined." However, most new-hire orientation sessions are knowledge-based and don't acknowledge the differences between the life they have left behind and the one they are entering.

You might have inspiring videos and presentations on your company's rich history and bright future, but do any of your presentations show the difference between college life and corporate life and offer suggestions on how to make the mental and practical shift? Millennials are more likely to bail on your company because they have a hard time committing to that dreaded 8:00 a.m. start time now that they have to drive through traffic rather than walk across campus. And that's just one of the adjustments they will have to make.

If your company has some form of an orientation program for newly hired employees or one specifically designed for Millennials, your goal to effectively integrate these new employees into your work culture may fail terribly unless you establish ongoing dialog. Over the years companies have launched internal programs to address the needs of certain minority or gender groups within their company for both development and retention purposes. With the distinct differences observed in the generational groups in the workplace, maybe it's time to devote more time and resources to this growing challenge. Companies such as Deloitte LLP, Brown Brothers Harriman, Sodexo, Marriott and Raytheon have all implemented programs to promote engagement and interaction between the generations, addressing workplace challenges, career aspirations and development needs.[1] The following are examples of the types of ongoing programs that have been developed to orient Millennials to their new normal:

- Regularly scheduled speaker series on topics covering a wide range of intergenerational workplace challenges, career opportunities and employee expectations.

- Networking events within the company to build and strengthen work relationships, mentoring and learning opportunities. These events can be planned as formal or informal settings or through community volunteer activities.

- Millennial generation councils that work with senior leadershlp to identıty, address and respond to workplace challenges, development opportunities, retention issues and work redesign.

- Leadership development programs that leverage social media tools, incorporate networking opportunities, and encourage mentoring relationships.

- Structured rotational assignments in targeted business units to expand workplace skills and professional networks. These rotational tracks provide participants, particularly Millennial-aged employees, with a practical overview of each business unit's goals, strategies and challenges.

The primary focus of these best practices is simply to integrate Millennials into their new work culture. When Millennials feel included, are given a voice, are respected, encouraged, and are allowed to fully participate, the transition from college life to a work culture is far less severe and opens their eyes to career aspirations consistent with their desire for a meaningful, purposeful work life.

Teach workplace etiquette

In an online article for *Forbes*, author Jeanne C. Meister noted surprising questions Millennials asked during job interviews. Nearly 1,200 managers from various companies reported some of the inappropriate questions they had to answer:

"Do I have to show up for work every day?"

"Do you drug test—often?"

"Can my Mom call you about the benefits package?"[2]

To your average Traditionalist, Baby Boomer or Gen Xer, adapting to office protocol is just the normal part of working with other people. Not so for some Millennials. According to Gail McDaniel, a corporate consultant and career coach for college students, it's the other way around. She notes that parents and teachers adapted to their needs for years. "Going into the workplace, they have an expectation that companies will adapt for them, too."[3]

So what do you do if your new batch of Millennials send text messages to their friends or post comments on Facebook and Twitter all through your meetings, consistently take 1.5 hour lunch breaks, or fail to meet deadlines? What if they respond with "You didn't remind me," when challenged, take naps in the break room (complete with snoring), over-customize their workstations with all sorts of clashing adornments or turn up their iPod so loud the people three cubes away can hear the music? If this happens in your work location, as it does in others, you have an etiquette problem. The head-on confrontational approach might work for some but for most Millennials, they grew up with constant positive encouragement and are not comfortable with critical feedback.

Every generation is annoyed with some of the habits or practices of younger or older generations and that is not likely to change regardless of the approach you take. However, if you borrow some of the lessons learned in a previous chapter on communication, the "why" is at least a place to start. Discussing workplace etiquette in an open forum can ease the tension and conflict between generations who get irritated at generational peculiarities. Add a little humor to the discussion and allow each generation to laugh collectively at the other's idiosyncrasies and you just might get people thinking twice before they engage in some annoying habit.

Managers who make "etiquette training" a fun experience and less of a "demand for adherence to office policies" are more likely to help curb annoying behaviors while promoting positive attitudes. Consider highlighting some of these office no-no's with the use of video, light-hearted presentations, skits, posters or other such means—formats consistent with the lifestyles of your new Millennial employees.

These first two approaches to Millennial development are geared toward helping them acclimate to this foreign culture they have entered. There are, of course, additional training needs once they have settled in past the orientation period.

Provide essential skill training

In an upcoming chapter we'll look at some of the skill areas where Millennials thrive. Here, let's focus on the skill areas for which they will need some help. These are essential workplace skills that can't be ignored or assumed they have brought with them to the job. Millennials will welcome this training. More than one out of five choose training as the most important benefit an employer can offer and two thirds say that professional development is key in their career choices.[4] So when you offer additional training opportunities, you won't hear many groans coming from this age group.

Technology has indeed reduced or eliminated certain jobs previously performed by people and will continue to do so into the future. But make no mistake, in any business, there will always be people thrown together to interact, plan, make decisions, collaborate, innovate and take action on strategies. Without strong people skills, conflicts will increase and hinder the growth and productivity potential of any organization.

Millennials must learn how to work with teams in both an assertive manner while remaining diplomatic. They have lots of experience working in teams while in school but working with a multi-generational team where the stakes are much different than their final grade will be a new experience. They must also learn how to deal with feedback—positive and negative—and how to set long- and short-term goals.

Time management is another teachable topic. Millennials may have mastered how to manage their time around part-time jobs, study habits and their social life, but now more of their parameters are being set by their employer which takes some of the control out of their hands. So how do they manage these new schedules? They have grown up in a diverse culture in terms of race, but add multiple generations to the mix, a variety of perspectives philosophically, politically, economically and socially, and Millennials will be confronted with new challenges.

Much has been said about Millennials' widespread use of social media tools and smart phones to communicate with their network of friends. In many ways their comfort level with such tools can be leveraged as a strength. However, they will need guidance in what is appropriate communication in the workplace.

If you've ever browsed through a Millennial-age student's Facebook, Twitter or Instagram account, most likely you'll find a collection of photos and "selfies" that would embarrass their parents and even raise a few eyebrows of their friends. Not all of them know that such self indulgent behavior is not appropriate for the professional workplace and will need to be coached in what is allowable and what crosses the line. To them it might be considered light-hearted humor and even tame compared to some of the content that has gone viral. Having an open and frank conversation about the type of content that will result in disciplinary action should be conducted early in their employment and periodically to ensure that such behavior is controlled and prevented.

Adapt to their learning style

Here's a little assignment: If you know any Millennial-age employees or if you have sons, daughters, nieces or nephews, ask them a question like this, "If you wanted to teach yourself how to play guitar, piano, learn how to tie a neck tie, make a tie-dyed shirt (or virtually any other 'How to' type question), how would you go about it"? Most likely you'll hear one of two responses:

"I would Google it."

"I would look for it on YouTube."

We all know the internet is filled with information on just about every subject under the sun but Millennials understand that in a practical, experiential way. They used the internet all through school to help with science projects, research for writing assignments, graphics for art projects or presentations, word definitions, "fix it" questions and all sorts of other learning needs. So when they get to their new work location and their managers sense they need to learn some new skills, they are sent to a class. The classroom definitely has its advantages if structured effectively, but some of the best just-in-time training can take place with just a few mouse clicks with their PC or the smart phone in their pocket.

Training managers who want to see significant results and response rates from their company's Millennial workforce should actively pursue a database of training resources that are available on the internet—many of which are free. And if you have a hard time finding good material, give that assignment to an eager young Millennial who will turn up all kinds of material that once the training manager has reviewed and approved, will provide valuable content to guide Millennials along a structured learning path.

If you develop your own learning tools, make sure you include a heavy portion of e-learning and other technology-based tools. General Electric uses gaming technology to educate prospective employees about the company's values.[5] Such tools are ideal for a generation whose hands fit around a game controller like a form-fitted glove. E-learning methodologies are not only consistent with Millennials' training processes in school, they also provide flexible learning opportunities that fit perfectly with their desire to manage all their activities. That means they are likely to take an e-learning course on creative thinking while lounging at the local Starbucks. For them, that's the best scenario possible.

Train them in team environments

Of course not all the learning will take place with their faces glued to a YouTube video or logging responses to questions on an e-learning program. Knowledge needs to be processed and assimilated into real-world situations and in the context of your work goals and expectations. Throughout their school years they learned to work on projects in teams where each had different assignments. As soon as you can, place them on a team, give them specific tasks to tackle and let them work side-by-side with more seasoned veterans who can offer experienced insights from the company's perspective. Make sure the assigned tasks present challenges rather than patronize them with token assignments that contribute nothing of great importance to the success of the project, the company, or to them personally.

These team environments also give managers and other employees from all generations the opportunity to see the strengths and perspectives Millennials bring to the organization. IDEO, the world renown design firm, is well known for how they assemble new project teams. They strategically select employees with various backgrounds, disciplines, and perspectives so a thorough, balanced approach is taken to solving creative problems. Millennials bring a youthful perspective that could be easily overlooked by older generations. Ask for their input, suggestions and ideas on areas such as technology, social media, youth culture and other topics and they will become willing and eager participants.

Don't forget about mentoring

Mentoring relationships contribute many benefits for both companies and the Millennials who are being trained. Bellevue University's Human Capital Lab conducted a study for Sun Microsystems and found that Millennials involved in a mentoring program had a 23 percent higher retention rate than non-participants.[6] Here's the part that will cause your CFO to salivate: the result of their mentoring program saved $6.7 million in hiring and training costs!

As the demographics of the workforce shift towards a higher percentage of Millennials, mentoring cannot be considered an option, but rather must become a leadership priority. Bob Canalosi, Chief Learning Officer of General Electric Health Care, stresses mentoring as a top leadership competency. He states that leaders need to become a "legendary builder of people and teams." This, he explains, involves "coaching and mentoring both face-to-face and virtually; challenging people to achieve more than they believed they could."[7] Mentoring, at its core, is a relationship between an experienced employee and one with less experience. It is an investment of time and energy into another person.

When Millennials enter the workforce, they are looking for mentoring opportunities. They've had that with their parents, teachers, coaches and other community leaders and they are surprised when no one "takes them under their wing" to guide, counsel and direct them in their career. In a poll cited by the Harvard Business Review, four of the top five characteristics Millennials want from their boss involved an active participation in career guidance and development mostly accomplished through mentoring. In order, the characteristics they look for in a boss are:

- Will help me with my career path

- Will give me straight feedback

- Will mentor and coach me

- Will sponsor me for formal development programs

- Is comfortable with flexible schedules[8]

Mentoring creates strong bonds within the workplace. Most business leaders acknowledge that when strong relationships are formed through mentoring, employees on the receiving end are far less likely to "leave their mentor" than they are to leave the company.

Reverse mentoring

If you want to double the benefits of your mentoring program, consider an approach that many companies have implemented: reverse mentoring. As stated throughout this book, Millennials want to be respected and included in the business process. They want to be heard and contribute to the company's success. Reverse mentoring gives them the opportunity to do that while strengthening workplace relationships even further.

Jack Welch instituted a reverse mentoring process at GE years ago when he sensed the need for his older workforce to become more web-savvy. More than 500 of his top executives were paired with younger employees to teach them about the web so they could gain a greater understanding of the growing trend in e-business. Other companies have followed GE's lead so older employees can learn about new technologies, pop culture, social media marketing and other business trends that influence market opportunities.

The concept of reverse mentoring might be a new idea to business leaders but it is a natural phenomenon that occurs throughout history. What parent at some point in their home has not asked their child how to program a VCR, set up the PlayStation 3, attach a document to an email or upload a picture to Facebook? Why not take this natural occurrence of reverse mentoring and make it work in your company?

Reverse mentoring can work in one-to-one relationships or group situations where open sharing is encouraged and every participant is considered a leader when sharing knowledge, experience and expertise. The challenge will be for older generations to set aside egos and learn from those many years their junior. Millennials will have to learn patience in the process as they try to teach skills that seem obvious and intuitive to them. When the focus for all participants is on learning, which helps all employees more effectively achieve company goals, a greater team concept will emerge and the barriers between generations will dissolve rapidly in preference for a more unified workgroup.

Encourage continuous learning opportunities

If your company does not provide or encourage continuous learning opportunities, most likely your company will become extinct and your employees' skills will be obsolete in a few short years. A popular YouTube video that at the time of this writing has gained over 15 million views, lists eye-opening facts about the rate at which knowledge and technology is rapidly increasing.[9] Consider these facts to put the subject of continuous learning in perspective:

- The top ten jobs in demand in 2010 did not exist in 2004.

- The amount of new technical information is doubling every two years. Consequently,…

- …for students starting a four-year technical degree, this means that half of what they learn in their first year of study will be outdated by their third year of study.

This presents a serious challenge for an educational system that attempts to prepare students for jobs that don't exist yet, to solve problems that will arise some time in the future. However, once students leave the academic world, the challenge shifts to employers to prevent employees from becoming obsolete.

Millennials welcome the opportunity for continued learning and numerous surveys have revealed their desire to forward their skills. They see firsthand how rapidly technology changes and are eager to keep up and add new skills to their toolbox. Without the opportunity to continue their personal and professional development, they will quickly search for companies that offer continuous learning as a part of their learning culture.

When businesses struggle in tough economic times, training budgets are often slashed or eliminated altogether. Any company must take necessary action to survive difficult business environments but when training is shortchanged, it could very well be to the demise of the company's future on two levels: Millennials will leave in search of development opportunities or they will stay and, in the absence of continuous training, they will increasingly become unskilled and inadequately prepared to address the changing business challenges.

There is good news here, however. There are some approaches companies can take to promote and provide development without acquiring crippling training budgets.

Vendor-based training is one alternative some companies have opted for when they are unable to sustain a year-round training department. These vendors provide skill-specific training on an "as-needed" basis and in the long run can be more economically feasible. Companies such as BESTWORK USA,[10] Kenexa[11] and Development Dimensions International,[12] are a few of the many companies offering customizable training courses and career development. Many of these vendors offer flexible and affordable options to address specific skill deficiencies within an organization.

In addition to supplemental training provided either in-house or through a training vendor, companies are wise to encourage employees to take responsibility for their own personal development and training. However, when a CEO or a department manager challenges employees to "be accountable for their own development," such seemingly motivational speeches can backfire when all the burden is placed on the individual. In resentment, some employees will accept the challenge, acquire their own training either through night or weekend classes, online training course, personal reading and other tutorials and then say goodbye to the company as they take their skills elsewhere. If your company is unable to provide the needed training for employees, another option is to grant them time to do so—on company time!

Google allows its employees to spend 20 percent of their time on projects of personal interest. The only stipulation is that the projects must in some way tie in and contribute to Google's business goals. Other companies have followed their example by allowing employees to pursue creative projects. Why not do the same with training? If you encourage continuous learning and development but then keep your employees so busy they never have time, what's the point?

So imagine this scenario: A company sets up a learning-lab with self-guided courses aligned with the company's business needs. Employees are encouraged to use the lab during normal business hours to further their skills. If the company tracks the courses taken by each employee, those employees can be placed or recommended for certain projects that leverage those skills for specific business needs. When other employees see the advantages and opportunities that come with newly acquired skills, they will likely join this development opportunity.

It is imperative for every business to stay abreast of the evolving business environment to determine what skills are needed to address new challenges. Who in your company keeps their eyes on the horizon for the emergence of new technologies, markets and unique problems that didn't exist five or ten years ago? Once these challenges are identified, companies will remain relevant and competitive by preparing and developing their workfroce through applicable training strategies. And, of course, when you do so, your Millennial workforce will be the first in line for the class.

Millennials work more closely together, leverage right- and left-brain skills, ask the right questions, learn faster and take risks previous generations resisted.

Mike Marasco

The NUvention program, Northwestern University

Millennials, for the most part, have grown up in a world full of possibilities and constant innovation, and their confidence, optimism, creative thinking and willingness to embrace new challenges make them an asset to your team.

Sherman Updegraff, blogger

11

Leveraging Millennials' strengths

•••

If you have spent time on the internet searching for help on how to work with Millennials, no doubt you have come across all sorts of descriptions, warnings and criticisms of this unique workgroup. Terms such as "self-entitled," "bratty," "whiney," "spoiled," and "arrogant," are all adjectives that have been used to describe this generation. You may even have met some Millennials who fit these descriptions quite well. Of course, if you look around and are honest, you probably know people in every generation who could be described using these same terms. What is often overlooked, however, are the strengths that Millennials bring to your company. Some of those strengths have been touched on in previous chapters. Let's take a closer look to see what you are getting and how those strengths can be put to good use in your organization.

They are pretty smart

They may have a lot to learn when it comes to real-world skills, but Millennials are some of the most educated employees in history.[1] They are also getting higher marks in Advanced

Placement testing, SAT test scores, and math and science courses.[2] Many of them are also seeking higher education in greater numbers than their parents or other generations. Although some analysts will be quick to say they are staying in school because they can't find jobs, regardless, they are acquiring more education while they wait for jobs to become available.

They know how to use technology

Their technological skills have been referred to throughout this book. Don't forget that this is a distinct advantage they have when you consider how much of our lives are increasingly dependent on technology. The popular e-Trade commercial with the baby in the crib who is "alone with his smart phone" isn't too far from the truth.

Whereas Baby Boomers and Traditionalists grew up with G.I. Joe dolls, Barbies, Tinkertoys and hula hoops, Millennials can't remember not having some entertainment device that didn't include a joystick, game controller, optical mouse or a touch screen. Their parents wrote term papers using typewriters, 3 X 5 index cards and multiple trips to the library. Millennials conducted research for their papers using Google while sitting in their room sending text messages on their smart phone with an iPod blasting the hundreds of songs downloaded from iTunes. In addition to creating their paper using Microsoft Word and then printing out multiple pages on their color printer, they may have even given a verbal presentation in class using PowerPoint with embedded graphics and videos all shot with their iPhone. So if your project team consisting of primarily older generation employees needs some help assembling a graphic-intensive, technology-driven presentation, you might want them to grab one of their new Millennial teammates and have them teach the old dogs some new tricks.

They are optimistic

In spite of facing a weak job market, Millennials are still optimistic about the future and the contributions they feel they can make. Maybe their optimism needs a little education, but it certainly doesn't need to be squelched. Their optimism can provide the energy some stagnant teams need to push themselves to achieve new products, services and strategies. The key is to balance the maturing process without putting out the fire that keeps them believing all things are possible.

They are good at multi-tasking

There is a lot written about the subject of multi-tasking. Some argue that multi-tasking is actually context switching because the mind is incapable of simultaneously conducting two cognitive tasks. That may be the case and there may be some concerns about the reduced attention required to carry on multiple tasks at once. Whatever you call it, Millennials seem quite comfortable switching back and forth between multiple tasks, and this can be a great skill to possess when working In an environment where they have to juggle several projects at once. Maybe it's due to all the video games they've played that require skillful eye-hand coordination while carrying on conversations with their friends. They've all conducted several instant-message conversations on their PC or smart phone while watching a movie they downloaded from Hulu. All their lives they have been bombarded with multi-sources of sensory information and somehow figured out how to keep up with it—or at least most of it.

The debate is still ongoing on how effectively a person can complete simultaneous projects when rapidly switching attention from one subject to another. However, based on the world they are accustomed to, if anyone is positioned to master this skill, the Millennials will probably be the first.

They know how to work in teams

Much of the business literature these days addresses the importance of developing high-performance teams. These books are filled with suggestions and tips on how to manage multiple personalities, how to encourage participation from all team members and ways to encourage conversation and ideas from the group. All good suggestions for companies who sense the need to get older, "lone ranger" workers out of their isolated work stations and pool their strengths and experiences in a group environment. You won't have that struggle with your Millennials work group.

Millennials grew up in an educational system that encouraged group projects and group learning. They naturally assembled in virtual groups through social media channels so the idea of complete isolation or constantly working solo is pretty foreign to them. Teams have become a much more popular approach to solving business problems or developing new ideas. Millennials enter your workforce already primed for such a working style. Don't wait until you think they have paid their dues, rather, place them on a project team to not only learn about your business processes but also for the contributions they can make to the team's objectives.

They are civic minded

As discussed before, Millennials welcome opportunities to volunteer and participate in community projects. With their experience working on project teams in the past, they can prove to be some of your greatest assets and supporters of your philanthropic activities. The energy they bring to such civic-focused projects can help boost morale throughout your company or department and also contribute greatly to the corporate citizenship image you are trying to project.

Community-based projects are also great opportunities to develop leadership and organizational skills among your Millennials. If you have periodic or annual volunteer events such as the United Way Day of Caring, why not let your Millennial employees plan and organize the event? This not only allows them to exercise their civic-minded muscles and coordinate a team project, it instills confidence in them and increases their worth in the eyes of older employees.

Don't wait to leverage their strengths

Traditionally, companies bring on new employees, put them in entry-level jobs until they have paid their dues and then progressively move them up to higher levels of responsibility. That still seems to be the intuitive way to manage a person's career. Unfortunately, many Millennials are not patient enough to stick around for that lengthy process. Truly, some of them will need to learn the realities of the workforce and that it's not "all about them." But there probably needs to be some adjustments to that traditional development mindset when it comes to leveraging Millennials' skills early in their career.

Amy Hutchens of AmyK International identifies seven critical skills leaders need to be successful in the next ten years:

- Leading people

- Strategic planning

- Managing change

- Inspiring commitment

- Resourcefulness

- Doing whatever it takes—digitally

- Being a quick learner—digitally[3]

Hutchens says, "Baby Boomers and Generation X-ers, while diverse in their own right, are often highly competent in the first three skills; Millennials are experts in the last three. When leaders create cross-generational teams, they leverage each generation's forte and break through barriers more quickly." When you combine the strengths of all generations, you take advantage of the potential your workplace has to offer NOW rather than wait until someone thinks the younger ones have earned their stripes. That thinking is outmoded from the "good ol' boys" days and needs to be discarded. Hutchens concludes, "While a Baby Boomer teaches Millennials how to make a well-reasoned, strategic decision (not a Millennials' strength), Millennials can share how electronic content management and interactive online branding opportunities through internet networks and apps can revolutionize internal efficiencies and external brand awareness (not a Baby Boomer's strength)."[4]

As the world changes at breakneck speeds, companies don't have the luxury to wait until someone has "gained seniority." When you recognize the strengths your Millennials or employees of any age bring to the table, by all means, unleash those abilities to more effectively reach your goals.

Employees who believe that management is concerned about them as a whole person – not just an employee—are more productive, more satisfied, more fulfilled.

Anne M. Mulcahy

They love being acknowledged as human beings, as well as seeing you, their boss, as a human, too.

The Muse, a Forbes contributor

12

Managers Millennials love and hate

•••

So let's say you've made changes to your recruiting strategy and revisited the internal workings of your company culture. You are now more flexible and appealing to this new crop of employees that you've studied so closely. As they come through the doors excited and hopeful for a promising career, your orientation and welcoming committee launches a carefully developed strategy to help them meld into an environment that is far different from the one they leave behind. Everything seems to be working quite well as the new Millennial employees are given their work assignments and introduced to their immediate manager or supervisor. At that point, one of two responses will determine their future. If the young employee loves his or her new manager, you will likely have a loyal, hard-working, productive employee. If the opposite occurs and "hate" more accurately describes the relationship, you'll soon be looking for a replacement.

Think about the worst boss you've ever had. Most people can remember at least one. If you have memories of a tyrant for a boss, you learned to endure the hardships, work through the pain, and vent every night to your friends or family members. The next morning you picked up your briefcase and entered the battle for another day. How likely do you think a Millennial-aged employee would survive such a boss? It's a pretty safe bet they will be out the door after their first ugly confrontation. And who could blame them? It's a different world we live in than when Traditionalists, Boomers or even Generation Xers first entered the workforce. In the book, *First, Break all the Rules*, authors Marcus Buckingham and Curt Coffman stated it simply, "People don't leave jobs, they leave managers."[1]

Bad bosses or managers affect all employees. However, they will have their greatest detrimental impact on Millennials. For the most part, Millennials have been raised and educated in a nurturing, high self-esteem family and educational environment. In an article for *INC.* titled, *The Real Productivity-Killer: Jerks*, Maeghan Ouimet lists alarming statistics about the damage bad managers create for businesses:

- Three out of every four employees report that their boss is the worst and most stressful part of their job.

- 65 percent of employees say they would take a new boss over a pay raise.

- Bad bosses cost the economy $360 billion every year in lost productivity.[2]

If that doesn't capture your attention, let's dig a little deeper. We all know some of the notorious things bad managers do that run people off and sometimes result in lawsuits and other punitive damages for companies—sexual harassment, discrimination, intimidation, racism, etc. But what about things they don't do that run people off or decrease productivity? The article cited above noted these top five flaws of bad managers:

- Fails to inspire employees

- Accepts mediocrity

- Lacks clear vision and direction

- Unable to collaborate and be a team player

- Fails to walk the talk

Employees who work for such bad managers, at least until they leave to work for another company, are disengaged from their work. Hopefully, they are not actively disengaged. Actively disengaged employees can actually sabotage their managers—they work at much slower speeds, purposefully make errors to make their boss look bad, hide when the boss shows up, confess to put in less than maximum effort, take "sick time" off when they aren't really ill, and take more or longer breaks. How's that for unproductive work, low morale and poor motivation? In essence, as Renee Sylvestre-Williams states in an article for Forbes, "Managers who don't create the right opportunities for their employees, don't communicate with them, and don't appreciate them often find themselves dealing with a high turnover rate."[3]

Unless you address the Millennial challenge at the manager or supervisor level, you may be fighting a losing battle. All the little perks and parties companies like to throw at employees to make the environment a happy place can never undo the damage done by a manager Millennials hate. And you'll never be able to thoroughly address the problem if you don't know how to spot and correct a bad-boss situation.

Spotting bad bosses

To address employee turnover rates, one approach companies have taken is to conduct exit interviews. When a person chooses to leave the company voluntarily, someone, usually from the HR department, calls or meets with the employee to determine why they chose to leave. These exit interviews can be good sources of information and reveal causes for a high turnover rate, provided the vacating employees tell you the entire story. Knowing that their new company may call their former employer, Millennials, or anybody for that matter who leaves a company, may be hesitant to trash-talk their boss for fear of a bad review. Others may not want to discuss their real feelings about the company or their boss and simply say, "This new job just offers more opportunities," or, "It's more suited to my interests and education." Exit interviews should be conducted when possible, but it's not the only indication you may have a bad boss driving up your turnover rate. Here are some other signs to look for when trying to determine if you have a bad boss in your company.

Higher turnover compared to other parts of the company

Employee turnover is an issue with Millennials in general, but if the numbers are out of proportion from other departments or divisions, it's worth a closer look. It could be the nature of the work in a particular division such as lack of development or unchallenging work. But the driving factor could be the boss who makes everyone want to run for the door.

High number of "sick days" for a particular department

This is a touchy subject. People do get sick and shouldn't come to work to pass germs along to co-workers. There are people who never miss a day and are determined to not let a simple cold or headache keep them from their work. There are others, however, who are well aware of the sick-day policy and will push it to the limit. It could be because the employee is just a slacker and will look for any occasion to miss a day of work. "Mysteriously," they seem to develop most of their illnesses on Monday or Friday. Another explanation may be the excess number of sick days taken in one particular department is because the boss is just making them all "sick." A high number of sick days in a department may not be the convincing proof that the boss is the culprit, but it's just one more indication that could point back to an unbearable manager.

Higher number of complaints from department employees

Yes, there are some employees who are just whiners. They will complain about anything that even slightly disrupts the world that revolves around them. But when the complaints begin to pile up, a pattern could be forming that could indicate an inflexible boss who has poor people skills. Managing conflict, personality clashes, disagreements, bad attitudes and other types of disruptive behaviors is a major part of a manager's responsibility. When the work environment in a department just seems to have chronic people issues in the form of complaints, either the boss doesn't know how to manage the team or is simply the cause of the chaos. Either way, a closer look at this boss is in order.

An iron-clad leadership philosophy

There are still some type-A personalities that insist on a "my-way-or-the-highway" leadership style. That may have worked in the past in certain industries. Even if people did hang on to their jobs for dear life, the misery took an enormous toll on them. If your company uses various personality or leadership style assessments, you should know who is operating with these domineering leadership styles in your various departments or divisions. Maybe the drill-sergeant approach works in some places but be aware that it could drive a lot of good employees away—particularly Millennials.

Poor staff development

One generally accepted definition of a good manager is one who does whatever it takes to make his people successful. The opposite could also be true. If people are not successful, show no signs of skill development, or don't move up to accept more significant levels of responsibility, it could be because a manager has failed to build into his or her people and maybe even sacrificed them for short-term achievements or self interests. Stand back and look at the different departments in your company. Which ones tend to produce the most "stars" compared to the ones who never rise much above mediocrity? Then take a look at the managers and ask why there is a difference between the two.

Declining number of people opting to work in a particular department

In college, certain professors developed reputations for being "the most sought after teachers." Their classes were the first ones to fill up and students would go to great lengths to find a way into their classrooms. Good managers have the same effect in the workplace. Of course, bad managers do as well. There might be some departments where the work is less desirable or even dreaded, but the style or personality of the manager can have a big impact on who wants in and who prays they never get that rotation assignment. Open your eyes. You know who is favored in your company and who is not. Ask why.

...

Most every company has some form of performance evaluation to determine employee effectiveness. These are helpful tools to further develop the skills and abilities of your leadership team. However, they may not always give you the most accurate picture in terms of the impact they have on employees' workplace satisfaction and fulfillment. Employee opinion polls, Employee Hotlines and other types of assessments can help to the degree that honest, open feedback is given without fear of retaliation. An objective evaluation of the above indicators can help identify who might in fact be driving your people away.

Managers Millennials Hate

By now you may have a pretty good idea of the type of manager that could drive away your young Millennial staff. Here are some specific manager types that will send your Millennials out the door to search for a greener pasture.

The Zinger

One of the favorite office pastimes is what some would term "delivering good zingers!" For most people, taking little shots at co-workers is all meant as harmless fun, especially for those who have been around for years and have learned to accept that as part of the territory. But when Millennials become the butt of jokes as the "rookies" or referred to as the "spoiled, self-entitled" bunch, those zingers will zap the life out of the young worker. They will develop great resentment toward their superiors.

The Micromanager

Most likely you've never met anyone who likes to be micromanaged. Millennials are no different. Where is the trust when a manager insists on hovering over an employee's work, directing the most minute details? And what's the point of even having an employee if the manager is going to manage at that level? Micromanaging shuts down innovation and personal contributions from aspiring employees who finally come to the conclusion, "Why try? In the end, my manager is going to change it anyway." Millennials, like most new employees, come into a company hopeful they can contribute and be recognized for their work. That's not very likely with an oppressive micromanager.

The Fire Hose

Imagine a young child running up to his mother with a freshly painted picture and proudly exclaims, "Look at my picture Mommy!" Mom takes the picture, studies it for a minute and asks, "What is that!? I don't get it. It's all wrong. One thing's for sure, you aren't much of an artist." Yeah, this mom probably wouldn't get many votes for "Mother of the Year." The problem is "mothers" and "fathers" like this get dressed up every day, head to the office and act the same way when they constantly shoot down or discredit the ideas and suggestions of other employees. Many seasoned workers can recall working for or knowing a boss who only accepted "good" ideas if they were his or her own. Remember, Millennials have been told they can change the world. The manager who constantly extinguishes their ideas like a massive fire hose will soon see those same ideas taken to another company where they could in fact turn into breakthrough products or services. Turn off the fire hose and help them develop their ideas into winners.

The Vacillator

Millennials do respect authority. They don't respect authority figures who are grossly inconsistent. As a matter of fact, neither do most people. Managers who constantly flip-flop on their decisions or conduct themselves in a disorganized, haphazard fashion do not instill confidence or facilitate the best work from their employees. Most employees become disheartened when the plans constantly change, directions are frequently altered and decisions are reversed. Millennials have no patience with such bosses.

The Unobservant

One of the greatest motivational tools a manager has at his or her disposal is employee recognition. Good managers are always on the lookout for talent and when they see it, they recognize it and put those employees in positions where their talent can be leveraged for the company's good. The by-product of recognizing talent is a motivated employee who works even harder to repeat the actions for which they have been recognized.

Oddly, there are some managers out there who seem to have a blind eye to the skills and abilities employees bring to the workforce—good work goes unnoticed and no one ever calls attention to the skills that are responsible for productive work. When managers are blind to employee skills and contributions, those employees feel unappreciated and will never perform to their full potential.

Even worse is the manager who purposefully chooses to remain silent and withholds "pats on the back" for fear of making employees over confident. Some might even reason that "Millennials received enough trophies in school and now it's time to teach them what it's like in the real world." Maybe they do need to acclimate to real-world situations but failing to recognize and appreciate talent and skills sends the wrong message. Ultimately, this manager will suck the life right out of employees who truly want to make a difference.

The Technological Klutz

We live in the 21st century. The workplace has dramatically changed in the last 30 years. There are managers in the workplace who can still remember what it was like to operate without a personal computer, smart phone or other such commonplace office tools. However, some are still slow to adapt and laugh off some of the latest technological developments.

Managers who cling to slow, archaic methods for accomplishing tasks when technology provides much faster and efficient means become the laughing stock of Millennials. Remember, this generation got their first smart phone when they were a teenager or younger. To Millennials, such managers seem outdated and unwilling to learn, grow and further their skills. They question why these managers should remain in positions of leadership when their technological skills are so obsolete. Managers who brush it off by saying, "I'm just very old-school," will never inspire confidence or gain respect from their young, techno-savvy employees who embrace technology as a normal part of doing their job.

No manager is perfect and even the best managers have their own particular flaws or weaknesses. The above list is not exhaustive but does highlight certain areas that drive Millennials crazy. Of course, when you study the list carefully, those traits probably frustrate other employees equally. But when it comes to Millennials, who are prone to job-hop in the early days of their professional careers, they will be less tolerant than those who have just accepted bad or quirky managers as part of the territory.

Managers Millennials Love

If you took all the traits listed above and reversed them, you would have a pretty good profile of a manager Millennials love. Let's look at these a little more closely and highlight some other character qualities that endear Millennials to their managers.

Manager as teacher and student

As indicated earlier, Millennials want to learn and acquire new skills. They respond positively to managers and mentors who will take the time to teach them. Ask most any employee about a manager or boss that had the greatest impact on their life and they will generally tell you about some advice or words of wisdom learned from a manager who took them under their wing. Their eagerness to learn is vitally important to companies whose Traditionalists and Baby Boomer managers will be retiring in greater numbers in the next several years. When you realize that by the year 2020 Millennials will make up 40 percent of the workforce, it is imperative you match them up with managers who will invest in their learning and development so they can successfully pass the torch as those more mature managers move into retirement.

Millennials also respect managers who have continued to learn and acquire new skills throughout their career. If continuous improvement is important to businesses that expect to survive and thrive into the future, then managers better model those behaviors by continuing their own personal education. Managers who are continuous learners dispel the view that some Millennials hold regarding the older, obsolete workforce. If you want Millennials to grow, learn and evolve, make sure your managers are doing the same.

Manager as collaborator

Traditionally, management was viewed as being figuratively and realistically separated from the rest of the workforce. Managers kept their offices in an isolated wing of the building and even those who were closer to the frontline tended to keep their door closed. This closed-door mentality represented an impenetrable barrier between management and employees. One of the downsides of this "us/them" mentality is the inability for both sides to benefit or take advantage of potentially powerful working relationships.

Tom Kelley, a partner at IDEO, a business that many consider to be the most innovative company in the world, stresses the need for collaboration if companies want to get the best and most from all employees. "At the senior management level in far too many companies," Kelley said, "there is this top-down attitude--the belief that all the worthwhile ideas are created at the top of the organization, and everyone else is just an implementer. The CEOs believe that they are better at everything than anyone else, and if only they had enough arms and legs, then everything would be more successful. The free flow of information up and down the organization is critical for innovation, but a top-down management style tends to severely restrict the emergence of any new ideas and inhibits the development of the 'collective wisdom' of the company."[4]

Remember, Millennials are comfortable with working in teams and throughout their education they learned to collaborate with their classmates. Managers who roll up their sleeves and work side-by-side with Millennials gain their respect and develop strong, loyal working relationships. If, on the other hand, your managers tend to shut their doors and issue work orders via email or through a chain of command process, the quality of the work produced will only be as good as the ideas and processes your manager hands down. These days, creativity and innovation are largely the result of a collaborative effort that comes from a multitude of sources, not a lone creative savant sitting in the back of the office cranking out one "brilliant" idea after another.

Much like the benefits that are gained from a diverse workgroup in terms of race and gender, when solving business-focused issues there is great value and benefit when perspectives of all ages and personality types are considered. When Millennials are ignored in discussions or are not included in the problem solving process, companies not only alienate them from other employees, but they rob themselves of the opportunity to gain valuable insights from these generational representatives. If you place most Millennials in an environment where they can interact, participate, contribute and brainstorm, they will rise to the occasion and be a significant team player in the goal achieving or problem solving process. Just give them a chance.

Manager as encourager

Millennials are no different that other people—they respond well to encouragement. Come along side most anybody, offer some words of encouragement and watch their countenance change. Anyone starting off in a new career will face a myriad of challenges and adjustments. Discouragement and frustration are the norm so a little word of advice, a well-timed pep talk or just a friendly, understanding chat is all some people need to pick up and move forward.

Managers who purposefully and strategically plan their conversations with Millennials demonstrate great wisdom in bringing out the best in their employees and strengthening workplace relationships. Conversations with employees should always be genuine, but as John Manning points out in his book *Communicate!*, a little preparation can make a big difference in the performance and attitude of your employees:

"Throughout the course of the day, you know you will engage your employees in conversations. Take a little time to plan ahead regarding the key messages you need to deliver regarding your work goals and priorities. This doesn't mean that all conversations have to be calculated and formal. It does mean that at some point during the conversations you will direct your focus to substantial issues that help move employees to the next level.

"If your conversation begins with the usual social pleasantries such as, 'How's the family?' or 'Did you have a good weekend?' make sure it ends with a thought to ponder, an action to take, a compliment for a job well done, a change in process or procedure or any thought that furthers the work group's goals or the employee's ability to perform more effectively. These conversations offer excellent opportunities to encourage alignment with company values, beliefs and goals which will produce the desired and productive actions."[5]

Encouragement and positive reinforcement are effective motivational tools to bring out the best in your employees. At some point in most every person's career someone offered a little nudge in the way of a kind word. If you are now in the manager's seat, pay it forward and do the same. If you are not inclined to inserting encouraging words in your conversation, now's the time to change your approach before your employees look for managers who demonstrate more human qualities.

Manager as communicator

It's hard enough for employees to survive in today's business climate with fierce competition both domestically and globally, but in the absence of clear communication and direction, it's next to impossible. Corporate America is notorious for its proliferation of jargon and buzz words—"Corporate Speak" as some might call it. For example, in your attempt to motivate or inspire your team to action, imagine standing in front of them and giving this little pep talk:

> *In order for us to actualize our goals, we must leverage our core competencies and drill down to the best practices most consistent with our corporate values. I'm asking you to think outside the box, synergize all your learnings, give 110 percent, grab all the low-hanging fruit and take advantage of any and all windows of opportunity. I know there are lots of moving parts here but hopefully you feel empowered, I have your buy-in and you are ready to move the needle. So, does everyone know what to do?*

If your boss gave this "impassioned" speech, would you know what to do? If your conversations are as cryptic as the above speech, one of two realities are at work. First, your employees most likely do not perceive you as one who gives clear directions. The above speech may sound impressive but what does it actually mean? What are the windows of opportunity? How exactly are the employees suppose to "synergize all their learnings" (bad grammar included)? With such ambiguity, what are the chances your department will move in the right direction much less achieve your goals? Slim to none. Second, if you or any other manager is prone to such obfuscation, it could be a sign that the right course of action is unclear to you. And if it is unclear to you, what chance is there that your department will ever move forward toward goal achievement? Again, slim to none.

Veteran employees may be accustomed to such lack of

clarity but this is new territory for Millennials. When Millennials work for managers who fail abysmally to provide clear communication and direction, it's one more reason why they search for new and better opportunities.

When it comes to communicating effectively with Millennials, or any new employee for that matter, a manager must always be aware of the "Curse of Knowledge." Throughout their book, *Made to Stick*, authors Chip Heath and Dan Heath effectively illustrate how the Curse of Knowledge can be a major impediment to effective communication. The Curse of Knowledge is simply forgetting what it's like to not know something. In the authors words, "Once we know something, we find it hard to imagine what it was like not to know it. Our knowledge has 'cursed' us. And it becomes difficult for us to share our knowledge with others, because we can't readily re-create our listener's state of mind."[6]

The failure to "re-create your listener's state of mind" is the primary reason most communication fails to connect with employees and especially Millennials. When Millennials begin their careers at your company, they obviously don't know what you know, they are unfamiliar with the corporate-speak used in your work environment, and as has been noted throughout this book, they generally think differently than all the other generations. Ignore these facts and your communication efforts will be disastrous! So, take a little extra time to connect with your Millennials. Don't assume they know what you know. Speak in more concrete terms without being condescending or patronizing. Then Millennials will respect you for your ability to communicate clearly and in terms they can easily follow.

Managers who trust and hold employees accountable

Trust is a foundational building block for all human relationships. Without trust, friendships, marriages, business contracts and any personal or professional partnership can not flourish, much less succeed. For trust to be an effective business strategy, two sides of the issue must be considered. First, there is the matter of trustworthiness. In the recruiting and hiring process, the ultimate questions the recruiter must answer are these: Is this person trustworthy? Is he or she who they say they are? Can they be trusted to do the job they claim they can do? These aren't always easy questions to answer without first hand observation and experience, nonetheless, these questions must first be answered before the person is hired.

Second, once a person has been deemed trustworthy, at least at the outset, now the manager must trust the employee to do their job. Managers who hover constantly and micro-manage an employee's every move communicate a lack of trust and create an atmosphere of fear and paranoia.

Now granted, every recruiter can recall stories of employees who "were not what they appeared to be" once they entered the workforce, so there will always be a certain unknown until an employee "proves" himself trustworthy. But even from day one, if there is not some level of trust between employer and employee, work will suffer and employees will feel as though they are under constant surveillance.

Regarding Millennials, building an environment of trust is key. According to studies by Deloitte, Millennials tend to trust their boss. One such study indicated that 87 percent either "completely," "mostly," or "moderately," trusted their boss.[7] Another Deloitte study found that "more than six in 10 employees (62 percent) who plan to stay with their current employers reported high levels of trust in their corporate leadership, while only 27 percent of employees who plan to leave express that same trust. In addition, 26 percent of those who plan to leave their jobs in the next year cited lack of trust in leadership as key factor."[8]

So, most Millennials trust their boss and they will stick around longer when trust is reciprocated. But how does trust happen? Trust is built and strengthened one transaction at a time. Someone makes a promise, regardless of the significance, keeps that promise and trust is established as trustworthiness is demonstrated. All Millennials want is to be given a chance to prove themselves. Managers who do that, who trust them by giving them more and more responsibility, cultivate fertile relationships in which they can grow and prosper.

Trust goes hand-in-hand with accountability. Without it, employees often default to mediocre work or laziness. Accountability is really about expectations and results—"this is what is expected, now demonstrate the results." Of course, that only works if trust is granted for them to produce the results.

Here's the interesting part of the accountability factor: Millennials have come to realize they must be accountable for their own future and outcomes. This is the generation that has seen their parents, aunts and uncles face layoffs after working decades in the same company only to show up one day and be greeted with a pink slip. They have seen pensions slashed, salaries cut, benefits eroded and opportunities diminished. They don't remember the days when the corporation cared for its employees from the first day on the job until the last day of their retirement (yes, when they expire!).

As they face an uncertain future, Millennials view themselves more as entrepreneurs who must take responsibility for their future and security—something the corporation no longer provides, at least in their minds. So the best and the brightest of the Millennial generation are stepping up to accountability for their actions in the workplace and are quite comfortable when their managers trust them to do the work and hold them accountable for the results. To do anything less communicates a lack of confidence which results in resentment and strained working relationships or broken trust.

Managers who welcome a sense of play

As soon as the subject comes up regarding a sense of fun and play in the workforce, many people roll their eyes and picture a workplace described by wacky, zany antics, party games, practical jokes and live bands where much fun is had but little serious work is generated. Zappos!, the online shoe seller, is known for its spontaneous, entertaining activities. Visit the Zappos! work site and you just might happen to walk in on an Easter egg hunt in one department while in the department next door employees engage in a "parade" through the facility clanging cow bells. At Zappos!, employees are required to spend 10 to 20 percent of their time "working" in such social activities that might also include trips to the bowling alley or the local cinema.

Now that might sound a bit radical for your company if you have more of a stodgy, somber culture. But even if you don't go to that extreme, what's wrong with just taking a few steps to lighten up the mood a bit so employees don't feel such a dread at the thought of showing up for another day of work? Susan Heathfield, a Human Resources expert, stresses the importance of creating a fun work environment as a means of managing Millennials. "Millennials want to enjoy their work. They want to make friends in their workplace. Worry if your Millennial employees aren't laughing, going out with workplace friends for lunch, and helping plan the next company event or committee. Make your Millennial employees happy in a fun, yet structured setting, and you are building the foundation for the superior workforce you desire. You are developing the workforce of your future."[9]

Managers who treat them like adults

Respect, or lack of respect, can be demonstrated in many ways. Speak to your Millennial employees as though they are children and you simply shower them with disrespect or, to put it in their words, you've "diss-ed" them. Although they may be young enough to be your child, or even your grandchild, please don't call them endearing little names like son, dear, champ, missy or other such cutesy names. This is not a little league team or a birthday party for a five-year-old. They may not show it but if you ever start a story with, "Well, when I was your age..." you can bet they fight every temptation to roll their eyes. Usually a story that begins with that line is meant to show how hard it was for you and how easy they have it today. What's the point? No two generations are ever the same and both have their unique share of challenges.

They may be as young as your children or grandchildren but whatever you do, don't compare them or their behaviors to your own offspring. How would you feel if they regularly said, "My dad, or granddad is just like you?" A little uncomfortable isn't it? If you want to be viewed as a working professional, treat them the same way. They are, after all, working for a living, are very well educated and quite capable of accepting responsibility. You may be coaching and counseling them in their new career, but you aren't their scout master protecting them on a weekend camping trip. It's more like you are all together on a wilderness excursion equally trying to figure out how to navigate your way through the jungle.

13

Before we go

•••

While researching and writing this book, I was struck by a recurring thought: Managing Millennials isn't really a whole lot different than managing any employee. Okay, that statement doesn't "undo" everything said in the previous pages, but it does call attention to some universal truths and some comforting thoughts in light of your perceptions of what is required to manage Millennials. Let me explain.

If you were to go back through the book with a yellow highlighter and highlight all the characteristics important and effective in managing Millennials, and then compile those characteristics into one long list, ask yourself this question: aren't these characteristics equally important to managing employees of any age? In most cases the answer is definitely yes! The point is this: managing Millennials is really not the daunting task you might have previously expected. There are, of course, some subtle differences in how you coach and counsel a Millennial versus someone who is a member of Generation X, but trust, effective communication, respect, collaboration, accountability, transparency, etc., are essential managerial attributes regardless of your generational mix.

That being said, if these characteristics are inconsistent with your management style, most likely you will struggle to have a cohesive, productive work team that truly feels a sense of satisfaction in the environment you have created.

Generally speaking, Millennials just think differently. In many cases, that can be leveraged to a company's advantage since they bring a unique perspective to the discussion that other generations aren't as likely to provide. Combine that perspective with their familiarity and comfort with technology and you've added additional strength to your team.

My hope is that through this book you have adjusted your perceptions of the Millennial generation and have a better sense of how to effectively work with them. At the same time, I hope this book challenges you to examine your managerial style in light of all the generations in the workplace, By re-shaping and updating some of your management techniques, you will not only lead more effectively but you may also be on your way to manager of the year!

Appendix

Although this is a book about managing Millennials, they aren't the only group of employees filling the cubes at your workplace. So the challenge will be to not only carefully handle the youngest of your workforce, you will also need to understand the differences between all those age groups and figure out how to get them working together in a productive manner.

Here, in condensed form, is a description of the other three work groups who will be working with your Millennial-aged employees.

The Traditionalists

The Traditionalists are those workers born between 1922-1945. Some refer to them as The Silent, G.I., or Greatest Generation. Many probably thought they would have all retired by now but that is far from the truth. When the economic meltdown occurred in 2008, the Pew Research Center Social and Demographic Trends project found that people in this age group who lost 40 percent or more of their retirement nest egg were twice as likely to remain in the workforce compared to those who lost nothing.[1] Some choose to stay in their current jobs while others seek employment in other "dream" jobs. The point here: Traditionalists are still working and many have no foreseeable plans to quit.

Now you might think that in this day of high-tech, digital tools—that were never part of this generations' vocabulary in their early or even mature years—these people just won't be able to keep up and will quickly be replaced by younger, tech-savvy, energetic employees. Not quite. Actually, Traditionalists are in high demand in some sectors.

Kate Rogers reports in a FOX Business News article that in May 2013, the unemployment rate for workers aged 55 and up was lower than for those ages 25-54.[2] In the article she cites Charles Wardell, president and CEO executive recruitment firm Witt/Kieffer who says people should not think of this group as the grandfather types. "People who want to work and are still active and have skills and experience are wanted by these companies," Wardell says. "It's not some kind of charity—they keep them on because they perform exceedingly well."[3] Wardell goes on to say that they complain less and don't have elongated career paths, making them attractive candidates.

Work ethic and values

Traditionalists were raised against the backdrop of World War II and the memory of the Great Depression they either experienced first hand or heard about from their parents. Those two events shaped their resolve to stay strong, fight hard against the most difficult of circumstances and sacrifice for the good of others. They learned to scrimp, save and prepare for the worst of situations. They learned to respect authority, trust leadership, put duty before fun, adhere to the rules and do whatever was asked of them. Reliability was a virtue high on their list. Who wouldn't want people like this working for them?

Relationship to company

Traditionalists see work as an obligation and commitment. During the Great Depression when jobs were scarce, those fortunate few who had them clung tightly for fear of losing their job and being unable to provide for their families. Their view of a "job well done" was based on how many hours they logged for the week. Quality performance was either secondary or simply assumed.

Many had a military background either personally or a connection through a family member and were very comfortable with the command and control style of leadership that was pervasive through much of the 20th century. It is not uncommon to find many in this group who boast of 30-40 years with the same company and proudly display the gold watch given at retirement. Now, as they remain or re-enter the workforce, they bring that same sense of loyalty to the job.

Traditionalists believe all employees should pay their dues and work hard to get to the next level. In social circles they often ask, "What do you do?" because they generally link their own identity with their chosen career. They typically don't share "their inner thoughts" because they tend to be very private on such matters. Opening up and being transparent was not thought of as being very "manly."

Relationships with co-workers

Traditionalists were raised in a paternalistic environment where they were taught to respect authority. Questioning their elders was unheard of during their formative years. That sense of respect for authority was naturally carried over to the workplace where they clearly understood their "ranking" in the organizational structure. Terms such as "reporting structure" or "chain of command" were common because of the military backdrop from which they came. Many of them were veterans and understood the importance of following orders from superior officers. Subsequently, they were generally good team players because they didn't rock the boat or initiate conflict in the workplace.

Because of their respect for authority, they are comfortable with rules and procedures and have a strong sense of right and wrong and the way things "should" be done. They prefer a command and control, formal organizational structure with a direct leadership style. Tell them what to do, when to do it, how to do it, and it will get done. No questions asked.

Traditionalists build strong relationships based on self-sac-rifice—what is good for the family or the organization. They remember the sacrifices of the Great Depression and World War II and learned to put others first over their own interests.

Like the other generations, they do like clear directions but they don't like to be rushed. They aren't comfortable with the frenetic work pace their younger coworkers have grown up with so don't expect them to multitask or hold multiple con-versations simultaneously on the phone, via email, IM and face-to-face. Millennials are good at that but Traditionalists consider that bizarre and impersonal.

Motivation and Recognition

If you want to show your appreciation for Traditionalists or recognize them for their good work, give them a plaque to hang on the wall, a framed picture of them shaking hands with the CEO or a certificate of completion when they finish a course. They'll always find some wall space for such me-mentos. And when you bestow upon them such tokens of rec-ognition, emphasize and thank them for their loyalty, experi-ence and hard work. That's what's important to them and what drives them to succeed on the job.

Baby Boomers

The Traditionalists discussed above gave birth to the Baby Boom generation—babies born between the years 1946 to 1964. When the veterans came home from the war and reunited with their wives or married their high school sweetheart, they started having babies, and lots of them—76 million according to most records. Whereas their parents were shaped by economic hard times, Boomers grew up in the post-war boom during a thriving economy. Their parents moved to the suburbs and for the most part, life was good and comfortable. Committed to giving their kids a better life than what they had, Boomers were showered with "stuff" and in many people's minds indulged or "spoiled."

When they were able to sit up on their own they were placed in front of this emerging technology called television. Sponsors wasted no time marketing to this enormous age group because they knew parents were eager to spend money on their little darlings. A whole culture grew up around Baby Boomers which eventually led some to label them as "The Me Generation." Eventually, this consumerist mentality wore thin on the Baby Boomers and their attitudes shifted to resentment and rejection of the "plastic values" they saw around them. The disillusionment and discontent reached the boiling point during the 1960s when everything was questioned and much was rejected. The Me Generation continued their focus on themselves and experimented in drugs, the sexual revolution, radical politics and philosophies alien to their parents. The heroes of the Baby Boomers include Martin Luther King, John F. Kennedy, the Beatles and Timothy Leary—far different than FDR or Winston Churchill who were admired by their parents.

Work ethic and values

Now in the days when Boomers were out protesting the Vietnam war, campaigning for civil rights or attending the Woodstock Music Festival, most people predicted that this self-indulged generation would never amount to much when it came time to merge with the establishment. That all changed in the 1980s when most of them took on serious jobs to make serious money. The term "Yuppies" quickly entered the vernacular (Young Urban Professional) as they exchanged their tie-died shirts and long hair for business suits and briefcases. They remained optimistic and individualistic and turned their energy into a competitive drive to attain titles, promotions and large salaries. They liked climbing the ladder because it represented upward mobility, status and more perks. And they didn't mind the long hours it took to get to the next rung—the rewards were worth it.

Relationship to company

Baby Boomers were loyal to the organization because they saw it as the means to their ends. Careers were extremely important to them and they appreciated the rewards and the status the company provided. They took pride in the years they poured into a company and were often heard recounting stories of how they paid their dues. To their parents, work was an obligation, but to Boomers it was an adventure and many of them were proud of the workaholic image they projected.

Unlike their predecessors, they weren't afraid to question authority or challenge the status quo. Harkening back to their days protesting on campus, they would challenge assumptions, fight for change and crusade for causes important to them. Boomers have never been afraid to shake things up a bit and have done so throughout their lives in all facets of society. They resisted the command and control style of leadership and were more prone to question the rules or work around traditions. Boomers aren't content to just go do the work as directed. They want to know why it matters, see the big picture and understand what impact it will have on them and on others.

Relationships with co-workers

Although Boomers are comfortable with a team-based approach, they also value peer competition. That sense of competition is part of the catalyst that drives them to achieve their goals. They are relationship-oriented and are not afraid to open up and share their thoughts and feelings. They prefer face-to-face meetings and in-person communications as opposed to remote technology.

Motivation and Recognition

Boomers like pep talks. They remember the speeches heard in their earlier days that moved them to political and social action. Align those corporate talks with clearly defined goals and action steps and they will be on board. They like to know they are valued and welcome wide, public recognition in front of their peers and in the company newsletter. The ultimate reward and motivator for a Boomer is an increase in salary and a prestigious title. Along with that comes the status symbol of a corner office and maybe a few extra perks thrown into the package.

Generation X

Generation X is the term given to those born between 1965 and 1984. This generation is much smaller in number than both Baby Boomers and Millennials. Gen Xers grew up on the down side of the economic curve. They watched their parents face massive corporate layoffs, an energy crisis, the AIDS epidemic and the space shuttle disaster. As the divorce rate reached its highest point during their early years, many of them were raised in single parent homes which led to the label "latch-key kids," meaning they had to go home from school and be there alone. They learned how to fend for themselves while mom or dad were off trying to make a living. Those who did have both parents living at home experienced both the blessing and curse of two incomes. The two incomes brought an abundance of wealth, which paid for college and expensive, exotic vacations but the long hours spent at the office and the lack of time spent together as a family put a strain on the parent/child relationship. Consequently, work/life balance became very important to them as they had their own families. Determined to shelter their children from the loneliness they felt growing up, time off became equal to, if not more important, than raises or positions.

Just as Baby Boomers grew up with television, Gen Xers witnessed the birth of the personal computer and therefore were the first technologically literate generation. They were also the first generation to spend hours playing video games. As they grew up during the media explosion, they were influenced by Ronald Reagan, Bill Clinton, punk rock music and athletic superstars such as Larry Bird, Michael Jordan and Magic Johnson.

Work ethic and values

As a result of their "latch-key" background, Generation X tend to be more independent and capable of working alone. They are very self-reliant, pragmatic and like to figure things out for themselves. They are the first generation to be more skeptical of the corporation than supportive, and are more interested in their own development than the development of the company. Who can blame them? Most of their parents and grandparents worked their entire lives for one company until that corporate job security began to crumble. Terms such as downsizing, rightsizing and restructuring became the norm. They saw it for what it was—layoffs and uncertain job futures. Since there was no longer any guarantee that the corporation would care for them from the beginning to the end of their career, they had to assume responsibility for themselves.

Generation X is quite comfortable with the concept of entrepreneurship. Because of their self-reliance, many of them prefer to work alone and don't require constant monitoring from their supervisor or manager. They like direction but they do resent intrusion from the boss, especially when they are told "This is how it MUST be done." They would rather figure it out for themselves or consider other options.

They are very efficient and intelligent and will find ways to shorten tasks through the use of technology. They enjoy skills training and welcome learning opportunities because it helps them increase their portfolio of marketable skills.

Relationship to company

Some perceive Gen Xers as being somewhat aloof or detached. This doesn't mean they aren't loyal to their work-place. They are just unwilling to put all their security in one place. Because work/life balance is so important to them, they aren't willing to "sell their soul" to the corporation. They will put in their time and work hard, but there are more things in life important to them than just their job. Their identity is not synonymous with their career but rather a composite of their goals, character, family and other interests outside of work. They approach authority in the workplace more casually than Boomers or Traditionalists and prefer flexible work hours and informal settings. Millennials are known for their multi-tasking but Gen Xers would rather eliminate tasks that are unneces-sary and inefficient.

One of the labels assigned to Gen Xers as they began to enter the workforce was "slackers." It was predicted they would have a difficult time surviving in the world of work and would never be as successful and as hard working as previous gen-erations. That's an absolute myth according to Alene Dawson in an article for CNN. "Compared to a national sample of all U.S. adults, Gen Xers are more likely to be employed and are working significantly more hours above average, according to the study. In Generation X, 86% is employed and 70% devote 40 or more hours to work each week. For those holding a doctorate or professional degree, that number shoots up to 50 or more hours."[3] They might like to work independently, but they do put in their hours to get the job done.

Relationships with co-workers

Generation X really has no issue working with others at the office, they just prefer to work things out for themselves. Millennials come to the workplace looking for mentoring relationships which does require a higher degree of supervisor or manager involvement. Gen Xers are well suited to accomplish the task without much supervision. That's a nice trait for your staff when resources and time are limited.

Gen Xers do tend to be more skeptical. If you want to gain their respect, demonstrate competence. At the same time, they are quite casual and friendly. They work to live rather than live to work so they are more interested in adjusting their work around their extra-curricular, "fun" activities. They tend to have a less competitive edge to them than Boomers so they may not be as prone to office politics and cut-throat tactics to get ahead. Because they are such competent, independent workers, they show a little more impatience with less qualified or unskilled workers.

Motivation and Recognition

If you haven't picked up on it by now, Gen Xers are motivated by freedom, flexibility and work/life balance opportunities. Time off is often a better motivator than "touchy-feely" public recognition. They do like the financial perks but are quite happy with a day or afternoon off to hit the ski slopes or the bike trails. They like and accept regular feedback, just not to the extent that Millennials crave it daily. If you need a project completed and your Gen Xers are available for the task, give them freedom and flexibility to "do it their way" without constricting rules. They like to wrap their hands around such challenging projects.

One interesting note about Generation X: They are about half the size as both Baby Boomers and Millennials and sandwiched in between like a middle child. Most of the descriptions of this generation, when they were discussed, was more negative which is most unfortunate. They are achievers and in the next ten or so years will replace Boomers and Traditionalists in leadership positions and will face some unique changes in the world of work.

Notes

Introduction

1. *Futurework: Trends and Challenges for Work in the 21st Century;* U.S. Department of Labor

2. *Futurework: Trends and Challenges for Work in the 21st Century;* U.S. Department of Labor

3. *Futurework: Trends and Challenges for Work in the 21st Century;* U.S. Department of Labor

Four Generations in the Workplace

1. Rich Morin, *"Most Middle-Aged Adults Are Rethinking Retirement Plans,"* Pew Research Center Publications, May 28, 2009, http://www.pewsocialtrends.org/2009/05/28/most-middle-aged-adults-are-rethinking-retirement-plans/

2. Kate Rogers, FOX Business News, http://www.foxbusiness.com/personal-finance/2013/06/11/older-workers-equally-productive/

3. Kate Rogers, FOX Business News, http://www.foxbusiness.com/personal-finance/2013/06/11/older-workers-equally-productive/

4. http://us.randstad.com/content/aboutrandstad/knowledge-center/employer-resources/World-of-Work-2008.pdf

The New Kids on the Payroll

1. http://business.time.com/2012/03/29/millennials-vs-baby-boomers-who-would-you-rather-hire/

2. http://www.forbes.com/sites/jacquelynsmith/2012/04/03/what-employers-need-to-know-about-the-class-of-2012/

3. http://www.pwc.com/en_US/us/people-management/publications/assets/pwc-nextgen-summary-of-findings.pdf

4. http://heri.ucla.edu/pr-display.php?prQry=19

5. http://www.careeradvisoryboard.org/public/uploads/2011/10/Future-of-Millennial-Careers-Report.pdf

6. http://www.forbes.com/sites/larissafaw/2012/07/19/how-millennials-are-redefining-their-careers-as-hustlers/

7. http://www.forbes.com/sites/forbesleadershipforum/2012/07/03/what-millennials-want-most-a-career-that-actually-matters/

8. http://www.forbes.com/sites/forbesleadershipforum/2012/07/03/what-millennials-want-most-a-career-that-actually-matters/

Recruiting Millennials

1. http://www.bls.gov/emp/#outlook

2. http://www.trainingmag.com/content/millennials'-effect-recruiting-and-job-searching

3. http://www.pwc.com/gx/en/managing-tomorrows-people/future-of-work/key-findings.jhtml

4. *The Culturetopia Effect*; Jason Young, 2012 LeadSmart Publishing, pg. 8

5. *To Sell is Human*, Daniel Pink, 2012 Riverhead Book

6. http://resources.dice.com/2012/05/23/hiring-millennials-tips/

7. http://www.flexjobs.com/About.aspx

8. http://www.bls.gov/news.release/youth.nr0.htm

9. http://www.pewinternet.org/~/media/Files/Reports/2012/PIP_Future_of_Internet_2012_Young_brains_PDF.pdf

Retaining Millennials

1. http://millennialbranding.com/2013/08/cost-millennial-retention-study/

2. http://www.youtube.com/watch?v=r3vXIbidSgU

3. http://resources.dice.com/2012/05/23/hiring-millennials-tips/

4. http://www.gorowe.com/main/what-is-rowe/

5. http://www.cbsnews.com/8301-505125_162-51237128/what-is-a-results-only-work-environment/

6. http://onlinemba.unc.edu/mba at unc-blog/geny-in-the-workplace/

7. *The Leader's Guide to Lateral Thinking Skills*; Paul Sloane, 2003 Kogan Page, pg. 2

8. http://www.ciozone.com/index.php/Management/How-To-Recruit-Retain-Millennial-Workers.html

9. http://carolinedowdhiggins.com/2013/03/motivating-millennials-at-work/

10. http://barkley.s3.amazonaws.com/barkleyus/American-Millennials.pdf

Managing Millennials

1. http://www.ciozone.com/index.php/Management/How-To-Recruit-Retain-Millennial-Workers.html

2. http://www.businessweek.com/articles/2013-03-14/the-misery-of-mentoring-millennials

3. *Communicate! How to connect, engage and inspire others through clear communication,* John Manning, 2013 Mannart, page 45

4. A more thorough analysis of the effects of a bottom-up approach to management can be found in *The Culturetopia Effect*, by Jason Young, 2012 LeadSmart Publishing. Results can be seen in companies that have far less voluntary turnover as well as financial returns.

Managing Millennials' Parents

1. http://www.inc.com/steve-cody/dealing-with-millennial-employees.html

2. *The M-Factor: How the Millennial Generation is Rocking the Workplace*; Lynne C. Lancaster and David Stillman, 2010, Harper-Collins

3. http://www.npr.org/2012/02/06/146464665/helicopter-parents-hover-in-the-workplace

4. *The M-Factor: How the Millennial Generation is Rocking the Workplace*;, Lynne C. Lancaster and David Stillman, 2010, Harper-Collins

5. http://ceri.msu.edu/publications/pdf/ceri2-07.pdf

6. http://blogs.wsj.com/juggle/2007/10/19/should-you-take-your-parents-to-work/

7. *The M-Factor: How the Millennial Generation is Rocking the Workplace*; Lynne C. Lancaster and David Stillman, 2010, Harper-Collins, page 28

8. http://www.npr.org/2012/02/06/146464665/helicopter-parents-hover-in-the-workplace

Motivating Millennials

1. http://www.smartrecruiters.com/blog/a-millennial-recruiting-millennials/

2. http://netimpact.org/docs/publicationsdocs/NetImpact_WhatWorkersWant2012.pdf

3. http://usatoday30.usatoday.com/news/sharing/2009-04-13-millenial_N.htm

4. http://www.boston.com/community/stories_to_inspire/articles/2011/02/01/volunteering_spirit_catches_fire/

5. http://www.boston.com/community/stories_to_inspire/articles/2011/02/01/volunteering_spirit_catches_fire/

6. http://www.huffingtonpost.com/2012/06/12/charitable-giving-millennial-generation_n_1590389.html

7. http://digiday.com/agencies/how-agencies-motivate-millennials/

8. http://www.adeccousa.com/articles/Adecco-Graduation-Survey-2012.html?id=200&url=/pressroom/pressreleases/pages/forms/allitems.aspx&templateurl=/AboutUs/pressroom/Pages/Press-release.aspx

9. *Society for Human Resource Management.*(2008, February).1 Workforce readiness weekly survey. Retreived from www.shrm.org/surveys.

10. http://www.shrm.org/research/surveyfindings/articles/documents/critical%20skills%20needs%20and%20resources%20for%20the%20changing%20workforce%20survey%20report.pdf

11. http://www.pewsocialtrends.org/2013/08/01/a-rising-

share-of-young-adults-live-in-their-parents-home/

12. http://www.dailyfinance.com/2013/08/09/millenni-als-money-student-debt-underemployed/

13. http://www.dailyfinance.com/2013/08/09/millenni-als-money-student-debt-underemployed/

Communicating with Millennials

1. http://www.timewarner.com/blog/posts/20121105-A-Bio-metric-Day-in-the-Life-of-the-Consumer/

2. http://www.timeinc.com/pressroom/detail.php?id=releas-es/time_inc_study_digital_natives.php

3. http://www.timeinc.com/pressroom/detail.php?id=releas-es/time_inc_study_digital_natives.php

Training and Developing Millennials

1. http://www.bc.edu/content/dam/files/centers/cwf/pdf/BCCWF%20EBS-Millennials%20FINAL.pdf

2. http://www.forbes.com/sites/jeannemeister/2013/06/04/the-boomer-millennial-workplace-clash-is-it-real/

3. http://online.wsj.com/article/SB122455219391652725.html

4. http://interactyx.com/social-learning-blog/millenni-als-in-the-workplace/

5. http://www.kenan-flagler.unc.edu/executive-develop-ment/custom-programs/~/media/DF1C11C056874D-DA8097271A1ED48662.ashx

6. http://www.kenan-flagler.unc.edu/executive-develop-ment/custom-programs/~/media/DF1C11C056874D-DA8097271A1ED48662.ashx

7. http://www.lindenbergergroup.com/newer_mentor_rules.

html

8. http://www.lindenbergergroup.com/newer_mentor_rules.html

9. http://www.halogensoftware.com/blog/millennials-continuous-learning-opportunities-are-everywhere/

10. http://www.bestworkusa.com/

11. http://www.kenexa.com/

12. http://www.ddiworld.com/

Leveraging Millennials' Strengths

1. http://usatoday30.usatoday.com/news/education/2010-02-24-millennials24_st_n.htm

2. http://themilleniallegacy.com/?page_id=42

3. http://humanresources.about.com/od/generations-at-work/a/5-more-myths-about-managing-millennials.htm

4. http://humanresources.about.com/od/generations-at-work/a/5-more-myths-about-managing millennials.htm

Managers Millennials' love and hate

1. *First Break all the Rules: What the World's Greatest Managers do Differently*; Marcus Buckingham and Curt Coffman, Copyright 1999, Simon and Schuster

2. http://www.inc.com/maeghan-ouimet/real-cost-bad-bosses.html

3. http://www.forbes.com/sites/reneesylvestrewilliams/2012/01/30/why-your-employees-are-leaving/

4. http://www.fastcompany.com/1838759/bring-out-best-millennials-put-your-coaching-hat

5. *Communicate! How to connect, engage and inspire others through clear communication*; John L. Manning Copyright 2014, Mannart

6. Made to Stick; Chip Heath, Dan Heath, copyright 2007, Random House, pg. 20

7. http://leadingwithtrust.com/2013/05/26/four-points-in-building-trust-with-millennials/

8. http://dupress.com/articles/talent-2020-survey-ing-the-talent-paradox-from-the-employee-perspective/

9. http://humanresources.about.com/od/management-tips/a/millenials_2.htm

Appendix

1. http://www.pewsocialtrends.org/2012/10/22/more-ameri-cans-worry-about-financing-retirement/

2. http://www.foxbusiness.com/personal-fi-nance/2013/06/11/older-workers-equally-productive/

3. http://www.cnn.com/2011/10/26/living/gen-x-satisfied/in-dex.html

About the Author

After earning a Bachelor's degree in Marketing from the University of Tulsa, Darren embarked on a career that has crossed several industries as well as continents.

Darren's early career was in the IT industry selling advertising and marketing services to some of the IT industry's biggest players including Dell Computer and Compaq Computer (now known as Hewlett-Packard). Darren left the IT industry to partner with two friends, starting a training company based on Southwest Airlines principles. After a successful launch, Darren and his family felt called to give a little back to society so they moved to Sofia, Bulgaria, where Darren became headmaster of a small English-speaking school. Four years later, Darren and his family returned to the U.S. and founded NexGen Leadership, a nonprofit organization dedicated to teaching leadership and life skills to high school and college students. While still leading NexGen, Darren later joined a leading auto finance company, first as Director of Employee Development and then transitioning to VP Culture & Engagement. After spending two years with this organization, Darren was driven to launch yet another new business, ProCulture Consulting which he still leads today.

Darren is uniquely qualified to write and teach about the Millennial generation. Darren is the father of three Millennial boys, has worked with many Millennials, and studies the Millennial generation as part of his NexGen work.

Whether working with managers or talking to directly to Millennials, Darren's entertaining and personable style allows him to connect and engage with his audience. His inspiring messages will motivate employees to work hard and perform at their greatest ability.

For more information about Darren and ProCulture Consulting, visit www.procultureconsulting.com.

About ProCulture Consulting

Want to participate in an in-depth discussion about managing Millennials? Want to train your managers on how best to lead and motivate your Millennial workers? Bring Darren and ProCulture Consulting directly to your organization.

- Managing The Millennial Generation
- I'm a Millennial – How Do I Fit In Here?
- Delivering "Wow" Customer Service
- How To Avoid The Coming Leadership Crisis
- How To Become A People Improvement Professional

Half-day or full-day workshops

Go deeper into any of the ProCulture Consulting keynote presentations by spending extended time exploring ideas and strategies. Each interactive workshop includes participant workbooks and offers attendees the opportunity to discuss these critical business topics in great detail, resulting in changed behavior and higher performance. In addition to the above topics, PCC also offers:

- Effective Presentation Skills
- How To Build An Employee-Centric Culture
- Take Your Call Center From Good To Great

For more information, visit PCC at:
www.procultureconsulting.com

Made in the USA
San Bernardino, CA
28 March 2015